KEEP CALM AND CALL THE DEAN OF STUDENTS

KEEP CALM AND CALL THE DEAN OF STUDENTS

A Guide to Understanding the Many Facets of the Dean of Students' Role

Edited by

Art Munin and Lori S. White

Foreword by

Bridget Turner Kelly and Robert D. Kelly

STERLING, VIRGINIA

Published by Stylus Publishing, LLC.
22883 Quicksilver Drive
Sterling, Virginia 20166-2019

Library of Congress Cataloging-in-Publication Data
Names: Munin, Arthur Carl, 1977- editor. | Stylus Publishing.
Title: Keep calm and call the dean of students : a guide to understanding
    the many facets of the dean of students' role / edited by Art Munin
    and Lori S. White ; foreword by Bridget Turner Kelly and
    Robert D. Kelly.
Description: First Edition. | Sterling, Virginia : Stylus Publishing, 2019.
Identifiers: LCCN 2019026230| ISBN 9781620368824 (cloth : acid-free
    paper) | ISBN 9781620368831 (paperback) | ISBN 9781620368848
    (library networkable e-edition) | ISBN 9781620368855 (consumer
    e-edition)
Subjects: LCSH: Deans (Education)--United States--Vocational guidance. |
    Universities and colleges--Administration--Vocational guidance--
    United States. | Student affairs administrators--United States.
Classification: LCC LB2341 .K367 2019 | DDC 378.1/11--dc23 LC
    record available at https://lccn.loc.gov/2019026230
LCCN: 2019026230

13-digit ISBN: 978-1-62036-882-4 (cloth)
13-digit ISBN: 978-1-62036-883-1 (paperback)
13-digit ISBN: 978-1-62036-884-8 (library networkable e-edition)
13-digit ISBN: 978-1-62036-885-5 (consumer e-edition)

Printed in the United States of America

All first editions printed on acid-free paper that meets the American National Standards Institute Z39-48 Standard.

Bulk Purchases
Quantity discounts are available for use in workshops and
for staff development.
Call 1-800-232-0223

First Edition, 2019

*This book is dedicated to the first deans of students,
the deans of women, who founded student affairs.*

CONTENTS

Being invited to write this foreword is an honor, because we greatly respect the editors and know the valuable work the contributors in this book offer to the field of student affairs. In addition, as we reflect on the pivotal roles that deans of students play in our lives, we are grateful to add our voices to the call for the importance of understanding more about this role.

Bridget

The dean of students of Fisk University lived in the neighborhood and knew my grandparents. During high school, my mother babysat his children. He was impressed with my mother and hired her to work in the dean of students' office the summer before she began Fisk University as a first-year student. That summer the dean hosted an off-campus retreat for student leaders on campus, and he invited my mother to attend. My father attended the retreat through his role as a rising second-year student serving in the student government. The two met, became friends, married after college, and are still happily married some 50-plus years later. This dean of students, taking care to see leadership in my mother, who was not yet a first-year college student, made it possible for her to attend a student leadership retreat and meet folks on campus, like my father, who oriented her into serving students on campus. She continued to work in the dean of students' office throughout college, became actively involved in student affairs through sorority membership, and worked in the dean of students' office at MIT at the start of her career.

In many ways, I followed my parents into student affairs as I served in student government and residence life when I was a college student. Fast-forward to now serving as a faculty member in student affairs for almost 20 years, the applications I review from those seeking a master's or doctorate degree reveal that dean of students is the primary position they would like to achieve. When my graduate students enter their graduate preparation program, they often want to know what they need to learn and do in graduate school to get them to the role of dean of students. There is so much to know and experience to be effective in the dean of students' role. I often do not know what to tell students to focus on in their assistantship and internship practice or what specific theories, articles, and books they should have at the ready. This book is a much-needed primer to help students understand the role and what they can do now to achieve dean of students' status in their career.

Rob

I remember being a student leader and observing who took time for me as a student, who answered questions, who treated others with respect, who led with a sense of integrity, and who offered feedback to me as a student, a leader, and a person at Loyola College. I remember that person was the dean of students. Eventually, when I made the decision to enter higher education through student affairs, the dean of students served as the model for how I wanted to lead and connect with the campus. As an undergraduate, I recall some administrators challenging me about my decision to begin my career in student affairs and forgoing the legal profession or pursuing a doctorate in the humanities. Administrators criticized the role of dean of students. In the moment, I do not think these administrators understood the influence the dean of students had on the institution. I have since come to learn that some who once criticized the role are now its biggest advocates.

Even as a doctoral student, I tried to better understand the role of the dean of students and the influence it had on students, faculty, staff, and other administrators. I read many books about the administration and organization of higher education. One text, *The Chief Student Affairs Officer* by Art Sandeen (1991), shed great light on this leadership role in student affairs. Quite possibly, this book on the dean of students can share more. Even in my own dissertation work, I studied how the role of the dean of students is complex not only because of the many audiences it serves but also because one's identity is constantly relevant. As a Black cisgender man, when I was in the role, my identities came into play, and I did not have a model, such as this book, to consult for guidance. I remember serving as an assistant vice president. New to the position, I sought to model myself after my vision of the dean of students. When I became a vice president, formally creating the role of dean of students was one of my first actions. I wanted students to see the title of dean of students, in addition to the title of assistant vice president, and know this person was there for them on campus. In retrospect, I have a deep appreciation of the complexity and joy that exists in the role. The role is so varied, so complex, and yet so needed and necessary. To this day I continue to see this role as all encompassing, focusing on student success, caring for the community, educating faculty, and serving as the conscience of the institution.

Need for the Dean of Students to Be Prepared

Perhaps it is because student affairs is often the conscience of the institution that it was a calling for both of us. We saw personally the transformative effect it had—Bridget personally through watching her parents work in student affairs, and Robert professionally as the dean of students at his alma mater, which helped him decide to choose a student affairs career. However, our realities as educators working in higher education for the past 20 years showed us how slow student affairs has been to respond to pressing demands: student demographics, market shifts, and learning styles, among others. If we are to meet these current demands and prepare for the future, we must act now. As a part of transforming student affairs practice, we need deans of students who (a) understand students as unique individuals with intersectional identities; (b) actively dismantle systems, policies, programs, and practices that treat students as homogenous or reinforce hegemony; and (c) put theory to practice in inclusive, equitable, and socially just ways.

Issues of equity and social justice are two areas, among others, where we need prepared and knowledgeable deans of students. Ever since we were in graduate school, we have been hearing about the time when the racial minority would become the majority. Educators did not address language about genderism and a spectrum of sexuality in our classes or in any tangible policies on campus. Fast-forward 20 years to the increase in minority-serving institutions and institutions who were historically White now classified as Hispanic-serving institutions. Gender pronouns, inclusive bathrooms, and identity-based centers on campus are commonplace. Students at our campuses are doing walkouts, demonstrations, and protests on issues as diverse as gun safety, police brutality, and immigration reform. The deans of students have their hands in all of these issues and the need to adapt depending on institutional context, location, size, and mission.

Conclusion

When we look around at the landscape of higher education with shrinking budgets and fewer resources, we are struck by the inability of some institutions to truly understand the role and value of the dean of students and its importance not only to students but also to the entire institution. This book serves to provide greater understanding of the role. The dean of students is a challenging role because it is often the one administrator thrust onto the front lines to meet students at their best and at their worst. The dean of students is advocate and educator, disciplinarian and friend, confidant and counselor, and adviser and parent all rolled into one. It is for this reason we need to understand more about this position and the leaders who take on the role. Students are best served when they can discern how they can use the dean of students and avail themselves of the resources only the dean of students' office can provide. This book is a window into this vast resource for students. This book may also help others who seek the role to know more about what they are getting themselves into and why it is so important that they are prepared when they take on the position.

Bridget Turner Kelly   Robert D. Kelly
Associate Professor of Student Affairs   Vice President and
University of Maryland   Special Assistant to the President
                                                        Loyola University Maryland

Reference

Sandeen, A. (1991). *The chief student affairs officer: Leader, manager, mediator, educator.* San Francisco, CA: Jossey-Bass.

ACKNOWLEDGMENTS

Art Munin

This book would not have been possible were it not for two people. First is Greg MacVarish, who hired me as assistant dean of students in 2006 and taught me more about this work than anyone else in the field. Greg, for me, has always served as the archetype for a dean of students. Second is Cindy Summers, who hired me for my first position as a dean of students in 2011 and taught me how to lead with dignity, care, and a healthy dose of humor. I also want to recognize the stellar professionals I have served alongside in deans of students' offices across three institutions. There are countless others who have been meaningful to me on my journey, and they include my parents, siblings, nieces and nephew, Vijay Pendakur, Ann Marie Klotz, Sumun Pendakur, James Stascavage, Georgianna Torres Reyes, Casey Bowles, Teri Bump, Rob Babcock, Bridget and Rob Kelly, Cheryl Green, Rico Tyler, Peggy Burke, Jim Doyle, Bob Wachowski, Maureen McGonagle, Fr. Dennis Holtschneider, Deb Schmidt-Rogers, Troy Johnson, Penny Rue, and, of course, Lori White. Last, each night over dinner I share the joy and difficulty of my day as dean with Vincent, Ava, and Heidi. Thank you for your love and support and for keeping me focused on what really matters.

Lori S. White

My contribution to this book would not have occurred without the invitation of my good friend Art Munin. I appreciate Art's conceptualization of the book, his serving as the book's conductor, and his deep commitment to the "*art* of deaning," which he demonstrates every day in his work with his students at the various institutions he has served throughout his career. I give much gratitude to the many deans of students who have been my collective role models for the position, in particular Sally Peterson and Randy Lewis at the University of California, Irvine; Jim Lyons and Michael Jackson at Stanford University; Penny Rue when she was associate dean of students at Georgetown University and the dean of students at the University Virginia; and Jim Kitchen, who hired me to be his first dean of students at San Diego State University. I am eternally grateful to my colleagues at the various universities where I have worked (go Anteaters, Hoyas, the Cardinal, Aztecs, Trojans, Mustangs, and Bears!) who have provided lifelong support and mentorship, an incredible friendship network, and the confidence to continue to stretch myself personally and professionally. I particularly appreciate that my current institution, Washington University in St. Louis, has supported my need to carve out time to truly be a scholar-practitioner. And NASPA–Student Affairs Administrators in Higher Education, my professional home for my entire career, has helped to create a sense of extended family within the student affairs profession and provided a platform for me to contribute to the field beyond my campus. My career in higher education and student affairs has been grounded by two incredible role models—my mother, Myrtle Escort White, and my late father, Dr. Joseph L. White—and been sustained by my husband and partner in the movement, Anthony Tillman. Thanks to everyone for their love and support.

SETTING THE STAGE

Art Munin

Having started college as a jazz studies major, I never had the plan of becoming dean of students. Like so many of us in this field, through chance and circumstance, you find yourself in places you could have never foreseen decades earlier. I first became assistant dean of students in 2006 and have worked as dean of students at three institutions. In the grand scheme of things, that is not a long period of time. Nonetheless, as I look back on my career thus far and all the twists and turns higher education has experienced, I see that individuals serving as dean of students have been front and center to some very tumultuous times. Whether it is dealing with student unrest, Title IX, crisis response, bias incidents, behavioral concerns teams, or campus violence, the dean of students has a complicated set of responsibilities in higher education. We are advocates, counselors, educators, disciplinarians, crisis managers, administrators, and cheerleaders, sometimes all in the same workday. We are asked to be many things and, sometimes, perceived to be more than we are. When I reflect back on my experience as dean, one incident stands out for when I realized the real and perceived responsibility the role carries.

In 2012, I was dean of students at DePaul University, and we were managing a protest relating to a tuition increase for the next academic year. This protest was fueled heavily by the Occupy movement that was sweeping the United States. This intentionally leaderless movement rallied around the sentiment, "The one thing we all have in common is that we are the 99% that will no longer tolerate the greed and corruption of the 1%" (Gautney, 2011). This evolution of the protest at DePaul led to a takeover of the president's office and then, the next day, the student center. I had been dean less than a year, but I felt comfortable in my role since I had been assistant dean of students and a residence director previously at DePaul. When I was called

1

to a large meeting room with many of the executives of the institution, I did not feel much anxiety. We all sat down and discussed how we could best manage the situation and support our students.

In this discussion I shared freely my thoughts on what I saw as the students' needs and demands as well as how we could best navigate the scenario. As the conversation progressed and the plan formalized, I saw many of my thoughts and ideas incorporated. That is when my anxiety spiked. It all of a sudden hit me that people in that room assumed I knew what I was talking about! What were they thinking? I was just talking out loud my thoughts; I never assumed that those ideas would be crystallized in a plan that was going to affect the lives of the protesting students and the institution as a whole or would play out on the nightly news if it all went poorly. It feels silly looking back on it now, but at that moment, I realized my voice mattered and the ideas I shared could have material consequences to a great many people, particularly students.

While that moment taught me a lesson on the real power and responsibility that flows with being dean, the situation also offered a reflective point on the perception of the role. As the protest moved from the president's office to the student center, I found myself sitting with the protesting students all evening and into the early morning hours. The students chose to move their protest to the student center because they were hoping to disrupt a vote on the tuition increase at the board of trustees meeting scheduled there the next day. I had many long and eye-opening conversations with students as they occupied the student center. While I disagreed with some of the tactics they were employing in their protest, I empathized with many underlying principles. I too worry about the cost of higher education. After all, I am a first-generation college student who, even now, still is paying down school loans.

At this point, sometime after 1:00 a.m., one student became quite animated all of a sudden. He raised his voice at me and asked, "Dean Munin, how are YOU going to vote on the tuition increase at the board of trustees meeting?" It took all I had not to laugh out loud. For him to think that I would be invited to attend a trustee meeting, let alone vote at one, was comical. I wanted to say to him that anyone who is attending that trustee meeting is not presently awake. In fact, I would be willing to bet that there is not a single trustee who knows my name. Instead, I kindly addressed his question. Nonetheless, it exemplified for me the perceived influence many believe that dean of students has in higher education.

The dean of students' role is one with widespread name recognition, and yet, few outside of those who have been dean understand what it entails. Students have their perception of an influential administrator.

Higher education executives can view the dean of students as the arbiter of angst or the dean of discord. Finally, Hollywood still clings to the long-standing archetype of the sinister disciplinarian. Regardless of this ambiguity, becoming a dean of students is a goal of a great many student affairs professionals in higher education. As such, with regularity, entry and mid-level staff will request a meeting to ask advice about their career trajectory, aspirations, and what professional development opportunities they should target. Invariably the question will arise: "I really want to be a dean of students someday. How do I do that?" While I always have an answer to give that is, hopefully, filled with helpful information, my internal voice is constantly stating, "I have NO idea!" After all, there are days I am not sure how I got here myself.

Unlike many other entities in student affairs, there is not an often-trod, prescribed path to become a dean of students. If you want to be director of residence, student life, career services, or campus recreation, the route you take is clear. However, the dean of students' office does not often have entry-level positions. It must be broken into at the mid-level point. How does a candidate accrue the skills and experience necessary to make that jump? And, furthermore, what are those skills and experiences that are required?

The path to the dean of students is further complicated by the incredible diversity of institutional types that exists within higher education. Institutions that are small, medium, large, rural, urban, historically Black, Hispanic serving, Asian American serving, Native American serving, Pacific Islander serving, low income, private, public, two year, four year, and so on—each institution needs its dean of students to be something different. In addition, the scope of supervision within this role varies greatly across the academy. Student conduct, advocacy, crisis response, behavioral concerns teams, bias response, Title IX, and a variety of other work responsibilities are scattered in varying combinations throughout our job descriptions. Furthermore, for some, being dean of students is the chief student affairs officer, for others being dean also carries with it the assistant or associate vice president title, and for still others it is a director-level position. In my three dean of students' positions at three different institutions, I had three unique experiences. Consequently, reflecting back on when professionals ask about how to become dean of students, my answer typically starts with "It depends . . ."

Regardless of the differences between dean of students' positions, those of us in the position have dramatically felt how much more complicated the role has become in the past 10 to 15 years. Moreover, the changes will only keep coming. When the new "Dear Colleague" letter is released, we review it to ensure compliance with our process. When the student protesters take over the president's office, we are the conduit between the students and the administration. When students die, we call their parents. When a controversial speaker is booked, we support the students hurt by the words spoken and defend the academic freedom that made the speech possible. This work pulls the dean of students in many different directions, sometimes opposite ones.

By no means is a dean of students doing this work alone. We are successful only with the close partnerships and work of colleagues across the academy. Whether it is campus police, media relations, residence life, academic affairs, athletics, counseling, or facilities, we depend on a great many others to partner together on the next crisis to unfold. Unfortunately, history has taught us that it is not a question of if but when that next crisis will occur. Regardless, a successful dean of students has to be not only willing to take every crisis call that comes in but also the one to get the call.

This introductory chapter would be incomplete if it failed to include all of the positive and rewarding aspects of being a dean of students. This position, because of its real and perceived scope of influence, offers innumerous opportunities to positively affect the student experience at the micro and macro levels. We are invited to sit at tables where major decisions for the institution are being made that will shape the culture of the campus. We also sit with students when they are at their lowest point and walk with them as they overcome, thrive, and find a strength they did not believe possible. Our successes are not recognized with an awards celebration at the end of the year. Our successes are experienced when we walk through the student center and see a student whom we served during a moment of difficulty. We often do not speak, so as to not draw attention to the fact that this student knows the dean. It is a simple nod and a smile that affirms the connection.

All of this introduction and overview brings us to the purpose of this book. We will draw together the diverse voices of those who are currently serving or have served as a dean of students to understand not only the functional nature of this position but also the lived reality of what it means to be a dean of students. A plethora of higher education texts cover topics that are embedded throughout this book, such as Title IX, crisis response, and managing behavioral concerns teams. However, when these topics are covered separately, we lose sight of the fact that each of these is occurring simultaneously in the work of the dean. There are some days I am deciding which case I am going to handle first: the sexual assault report that just came in or the student who made self-harm statements. As such, we are going to cover the knowledge, skills, and experiences required of deans of students today. Each chapter will end with specific recommendations geared toward helping current and future deans be successful in this highly visible and stressful role.

But first, before we can delve into where we are as a field, we need to understand how this role developed in the academy. As a precursor to this brief history of the dean of students' position, I want to share an often-cited quotation from one of this field's early leaders, Stanley Coulter, who served as the first dean of men at Purdue University. He wrote,

> When the Board of Trustees elected me Dean of Men, I wrote to them very respectfully and asked them to give me the duties of the Dean of Men. They wrote back that they did not know what they were but when I found out to let them know. I worked all the rest of the year trying to find out. I discovered that every unpleasant task that the president or the faculty did not want to do was my task. I was convinced that the Dean of Men's office was intended as the dumping ground of all unpleasant things. (Coulter, 1928, p. 37)

While many of us continue to be confused by our responsibilities as dean of students, there is solace to be taken in knowing that this is not a new phenomenon. I have often stated that whenever higher education encounters a problem that no one is really sure how to handle, it will often land on the desk of the dean of students.

History of the Dean of Students' Position

The very roots of student affairs, as a field, began with the advent of the dean of students' role. However, this is not a history steeped in altruistic service to students or in an effort to improve the campus experience; it is steeped in patriarchy. Higher education, as an enterprise, was founded for the education of rich White men. However, in the late 1800s, women became a more significant percentage of students enrolled in colleges and universities across the United States. In 1870, women were 21% of the student population, and that rose to 35% in 1890 (Schwartz, 1997a). The men in charge of higher education sought to find ways to meet the needs of this student population by appointing female faculty members to oversee their activities. Quite simply, "Deans of women were appointed to 'take care of the girls'" (Schwartz, 1997b, p. 518).

In 1892, the first dean of women's position was hired; Alice Freeman began her tenure at the University of Chicago following her time as president of Wellesley College (Hevel, 2016). Three years later she was succeeded by her assistant, Marion Talbot; thus, a new field was born. By 1911, fewer than 20 years later, a survey of 55 institutions revealed that 80% had a dean of women position on staff. As a further indication of the roots of patriarchy in the founding of the dean of students' role, "Early deans of women often accepted their positions after a failed search for a faculty position" (Hevel, 2016, p. 847).

Early deans of women sought to professionalize their newly created roles by organizing meetings and creating organizations. The first organizational meeting was held in Chicago and coordinated by Marion Talbot. All told, 17 deans attended from "the Universities of Illinois, Wisconsin, Colorado, Kansas, Iowa, Ohio State, Michigan, and Indiana, as well as Northwestern, Ripon, Carleton, Barnard, Oberlin, Beloit, and Illinois College" (Schwartz, 1997b, p. 507). By 1905, this meeting led to the creation of the Conference of Deans and Advisors in State Universities. This organization would be incorporated within the National Association of Deans of Women (NADW) in 1922 (Hevel, 2016). Another early milestone was the publication of the first book ever written for the field of student affairs; *The Dean of Women* was published in 1915 by Lois Mathews, who served as the dean of women at the University of Wisconsin (Schwartz, 1997b). Some of the sentiments expressed in this book still ring true today:

> The duties relating to this post [dean of women] have not been defined; they are in rapid flux; they are not the same in one institution as they are in another. (Mathews, 1915, p. v)

> In the whole matter of student discipline the cooperation of parents ought to be a thing upon which we could count. But too often warning letters to parents bring forth no response. (Mathews, 1915, p. 187)

> [The dean of women's] work has been conceived of threefold in character—administrative, academic, and social. Her problems have been presented as of two sorts—general problems of university life in which she has a concern and special problems incidental to the life of the young women students. (Mathews, 1915, p. 214)

This scholarly achievement, which has withstood the test of time, is a testament to the credentials early deans of women held. "By the 1940s, almost 90% of deans of women had a master's or doctoral degree" (Hevel, 2016, p. 853).

Deans of men rode the coattails of deans of women in creating a space for themselves in the academy. In 1909, Thomas Arkle Clark was named dean of men at the University of Illinois (Coomes & Gerda, 2015). This was followed by similar positions being created at Wisconsin, Iowa, and Purdue (Schwartz, 1997b). These deans in the Midwest hosted their first organizational meeting in 1919 on the campus of the University of Wisconsin and then, the following year, at the University of Illinois. This founded the National Association of Deans of Men (NADM). This organization underwent several transitions, the most notable of which was when it became the National Association of Student Personnel Administrators in 1951. This is, of course, the organization now known as NASPA–Student Affairs Administrators in Higher Education (Schwartz, 1997b). Having been in existence for 100 years, NASPA now serves more than 15,000 members throughout the United States and in 25 other countries.

While the early deans of women were, first and foremost, academics, the early deans of men considered their work to be a calling unique to those naturally born with the gifts to be a successful dean. "The deans of men became convinced that the most important skills necessary . . . were interpersonal traits and abilities" and "their intuitive sense of how to work with students" (Schwartz, 2002, p. 224). They bristled at the idea that their role could be taught in a graduate course or gleaned from reading a book. These early deans believed in apprenticeships to learn the role and fervently advocated that successful deans were born, not made. In short, "deans of men worked through force of personality, functioning as wise uncles shepherding older boys into manhood" (Coomes & Gerda, 2015, p. 9).

For some time, deans of women and deans of men worked alongside one another in parallel streams. They advocated for the students under their purview and expanded the responsibilities of their roles. However, this reality did come to an end. As the field of student affairs became firmly entrenched in higher education, these dean roles started transitioning into the vice president of student affairs position. These first vice presidents for student affairs assumed larger supervisory responsibilities within higher education, with a philosophy largely aimed toward student welfare. Although the deans of women had a field that was older and possessed greater scholarship, these women found themselves on the outside looking in (Hevel, 2016; Schwartz, 2002). "Former deans of women became counselors and senior counselors, or assistant and associate deans. Often, these women were reporting to men who were far less qualified and credentialed" (Gangone, 2008, p. 8). Our academic field rests on the bedrock of this patriarchy and all who work in student affairs today owe a great debt to these early deans of women. "The entire field of student services, from admission and orientation to student activities, to residential housing to career services, can be traced to the work of the dean of women" (Schwartz, 1997b, p. 505). Today, while gains have been made in closing this gender gap in student affairs leadership, the struggle is far from over. The increased equity seen throughout higher education today varies greatly depending on the type of higher education institution (Biddix, 2011).

Part of the history that shapes how the contemporary dean of students' position is viewed comes from Hollywood's portrayal of the role. For many of us, Dean Wormer from the movie *Animal House* (Reitman, Simmons, & Landis, 1978) will forever serve as the archetype for the stern disciplinarian dean of students. While this current generation of college students has less exposure to this classic portrayal, some of the famous quotations live on. I do not think a single semester has transpired in my career where a colleague has not invoked "double secret probation" as a potential consequence to student misbehavior. In 2003, this archetype was revived with Dean Pritchard in the movie *Old School* (Phillips, 2003). Any dean of student can attest that student conduct is only one part of our role. In fact, many of us spend more time on student advocacy and care than on student conduct cases. Overcoming the stereotyped view of the dean of students being authoritative and harsh appears to be a perennial hurdle. In relation to the pioneers of this field, Hevel (2016) wrote, "Many deans felt tension between their disciplinary duties and their desire to mentor and advise students" (p. 849). As is often the case, the more things change, the more things stay the same.

Keep Calm and Call the Dean of Students

The traditional "Keep Calm and Carry On" poster has been "reproduced, lionized and parodied around the world" (International Churchill Society, 2012) since original prints of it were discovered at a bookstore in England in 2000. Originally created in 1939, but never distributed, it was produced to be a motivational poster for British citizens in case of invasion during World War II. Two other posters preceded it, bearing the the phrases "Your Courage, Your Cheerfulness, Your Resolution Will Bring Us Victory" and "Freedom Is In Peril. Defend It With All Your Might" (Slack, 2012). However, nearly 80 years later, neither of those posters has captured the attention of the general public like "Keep Calm and Carry On," which yields over 1,000 items for sale on Amazon.

As "Keep Calm and Carry On" is a phrase that is often parodied, when we were looking for a title for the book, *Keep Calm and Call the Dean of Students* seemed fitting. In complicated and demanding situations, the dean of students should be a calming force. I have often experienced calls from colleagues who are feeling anxiety regarding an issue. Once I either walk them through a response or agree to take the situation from there, their relief is palpable. Building that trust takes an exceptionally long time; losing it takes only moments.

Deans of students need to be prepared to deliver in difficult situations, on a moment's notice. They must summon their talents at will and respond with dignity, grace, compassion, strength, and other attributes, more than there is space to list here. To be successful, a dean also needs support throughout the institution. I am forever grateful to have experienced such support in many instances throughout my time as dean of students. I hope colleagues throughout the academy have experienced similar support in managing the dean of students' position.

In tackling this demanding position, we attempted to bring organization to this complicated role through the structure of this book. To cover the following topics, we tapped into the expertise of our field. Chapter 2 covers the varying paths professionals walk to become a dean of students. Chapter 3 delves into the juggling act required as the deans of today attempt to manage an array of competing and complicated demands. Chapter 4 explores the different roles that a dean of students plays on campus as an agent of the academy and student advocate. These roles sometimes run parallel, and other times they are in opposition. Chapter 5 covers how a successful dean must strive for balance to be successful among all of the difficulties inherent to this role in higher education. Chapter 6 gives a 360-degree review of the dean of students' role by sharing the expectations that presidents, vice presidents, faculty, staff, and students have of the dean. Chapters 7, 8, and 9 are a series of reflection chapters from new, veteran, and emeriti deans, respectively. Chapter 10 seeks to draw together all that has been covered and offers thoughts on what the next chapter will be in the evolution of the dean of students.

Closing Thoughts

At the outset of this chapter, I shared a story of protesters taking over several campus locations during my tenure as dean of students at DePaul University. There is one final learning I drew from that experience that illuminates the impact of the dean of students' role. At one point during that protest, when the atmosphere became particularly contentious, one student rose to speak. She spoke eloquently as to why she supported the Occupy movement and all that it hoped to accomplish. She went further and challenged her fellow students to recognize that there were student advocates in the university administration working diligently on their behalf. She became quite emotional and shared that she almost left college at one point, and the only reason she was able to stay was because I met with her and provided support. This student specifically pointed me out from across the room and had tears coming down her face as she shared her thoughts. I was able to get over to her side of the room to give her a hug and thank her for such kind words.

Here is the learning from that moment—I had no idea who this student was. Before you think too ill of me, I would ask that you consider the fact that DePaul had 25,000 students, and I had been in the dean of students' office for years at that point. I cannot even begin to calculate the number of students I provided assistance to and advocacy for in all those years. Nevertheless, the central learning I took away was that the dean of students has the ability to positively affect the lives of students in ways that we may not even fully appreciate. A simple appointment on our schedule can have far-reaching ramifications. Our service, advocacy, care, support, and guidance live on long after those interactions. Lori White and I hope this book helps those who are currently on or will someday embark on this journey.

References

Biddix, J. P. (2011). "Stepping stones": Career paths to the SSAO for men and women at four-year institutions. *Journal of Student Affairs Research and Practice, 48*(4), 443–461.

Coomes, M. D., & Gerda, J. J. (2015). A long and honorable history": Student affairs in the United States. In G. S. McCellan & J. Stringer (Eds.), *The handbook of student affairs administration* (4th ed., pp. 3–23). San Francisco, CA: Jossey-Bass.

Coulter, S.pp. (1928). The role of the dean of men. In *Secretarial notes of the 10th annual conference of the National Association of Deans of Men* (pp. 36–38). Lawrence, KS: Republican Publishing Company.

Gangone, L. M. (2008). The national association for women in education: An enduring legacy. *Journal About Women in Higher Education, 1*(1), 3–24.

Gautney, H. (2011). What is occupy Wall Street? The history of leaderless movements. *The Washington Post.* Retrieved from https://www.washingtonpost.com/national/on-leadership/what-is-occupy-wall-street-the-history-of-leaderless-movements/2011/10/10/gIQAwkFjaL_story.html?noredirect=on&utm_term=.479d32a304e2

Hevel, M. S. (2016). Toward a history of student affairs: A synthesis of research, 1996–2015. *Journal of College Student Development, 57*(7), 844–862.

International Churchill Society. (2012). Keep calm and carry on, the real story. Retrieved from https://winstonchurchill.org/publications/churchill-bulletin/bulletin-045-mar-2012/keep-calm-and-carry-on-the-real-story-1/

Mathews, L. K. (1915). *The dean of women.* Boston, MA: Houghton Mifflin.

Phillips, T. (Director). (2003). *Old school.* Universal City, CA: Dreamworks Pictures.

Reitman, I. (Producer), Simmons, M. (Producer), & Landis, J. (Director). (1978). *Animal house.* Universal City, CA: Universal Pictures.

Schwartz, R. A. (1997a). How deans of women became men. *The Review of Higher Education, 20*(4), 419–436.

Schwartz, R. A. (1997b). Reconceptualizing the leadership roles of women in higher education: A brief history on the importance of deans of women. *Journal of Higher Education, 68*(5), 502–522.

Schwartz, R. A. (2002). The rise and demise of deans of men. *The Review of Higher Education, 26*(2), 217–239.

Slack, C. (2012). Keep Calm and Carry On . . . to the bank: Original wartime poster shows up on Antiques Roadshow Daily mail. Retrieved from http://www.dailymail .co.uk/news/article-2105518/Keep-calm-carry-Only-surviving-stash-original-iconic-poster-appears-Antiques-Roadshow.html

2

THE ROADS TRAVELED

On Becoming a Dean of Students

Jacob Diaz, Adam Goldstein, and Lauren Scott Rivera

> *Two roads diverged in a wood, and I—*
> *I took the one less traveled by.*
> *And that has made all the difference.*
> —Robert Frost (1916)

As deans of students who have traveled different roads to get to our positions, we appreciate how the roads—that is, the formal educational pathways, myriad opportunities and experiences, and ongoing professional development—have prepared us to serve in an important and increasingly complex role within colleges and universities. Before delving further into this chapter, we each offer a brief overview about who we are and our path to the deanship in hopes that readers will be able to relate in some way and understand the lenses with which we explore the roads traveled to this unique position.

I completed high school having decided that college was out of reach for me given that I did not possess the grade point average to successfully matriculate. Thankfully, the faculty and staff at the community college I attended restored my belief in myself and my abilities as a learner. As a Chicano, first-generation college graduate from the southwestern United States, I dreamt of becoming a dean of students since I completed my undergraduate degree. As a student, I experienced many of the challenges that come with being new to the college environment. I also benefited from the unwavering support of faculty and student affairs administrators who cultivated the seed of possibility that I too could someday contribute positively to the lives of college students who doubt their place or may not be considered as worthy as other students because of the dynamics of oppression.

Having identified my calling, I decided it was important to pursue a master's degree in higher education and student affairs administration and a doctorate of education degree in educational leadership and policy studies. Early on, I learned that to be a viable candidate for the dean of students' role, I needed to acquire graduate-level training and engage in professional experiences that would prepare me for the myriad complex administrative and student issues that deans face. My career began as an assistant director of student conduct at a midsize public land-grant institution, but within a year, I was asked to serve as the director. Both roles provided tangible, weighty experiences that informed my leadership style and shaped how I work with students and colleagues today. (Jacob Diaz, MEd, EdD)

My decision to pursue a career in student affairs came after a week of meeting with my undergraduate role models and mentors. It was two months after graduation, and I had returned to campus to ask big questions: "Do you feel fulfilled by the work you do? Do you believe you are making a positive difference in the lives of others? What is the hardest (and best) part of this work for you? Are you able to support your family and plan for the future?" I met with them individually, and each responded as I knew they would—directly, honestly, and in a way that helped me understand the complexity, hardships, and richness of the life and work they had chosen. I knew them as principled people who believed strongly in aligning their values and actions. I realized they were living the life I wanted to live. One of them helped open the door to a strong graduate program, and I walked through it. My wife and I met during an icebreaker on the first day of our master's degree journey, and our experience as a dual student affairs career couple began.

My first position in the field was at a small rural public university in the Southeast. I had the opportunity to be a generalist and work directly with students in a variety of settings, including campus activities, fraternity and sorority life, and orientation. I loved the variety of work experiences and ability to collaborate with students, faculty, and staff to address larger community needs and concerns. After two years, I got married and moved to a large Northeast city where my wife and I found jobs that advanced our careers. For the next five years, I worked at a midsize urban private university as a director of campus activities and eventually assistant dean for campus life. After our first child was born, we moved back to the community where we met so that I could pursue my doctorate as a full-time student. Upon receiving my degree, I was competitive for deans of students' roles at smaller institutions yet believed I needed more experience with crisis response systems, student conduct, and program and learning assessment before assuming the role. I accepted an associate dean of students' position at a large public university in the Southeast. After 10 years of working with bright staff and graduate students, supervising and supporting large offices, nurturing a procedurally sound and learning-centered student conduct process, and managing a high volume of complex student crises, I knew I was ready to become a dean of students. I then waited for the right community and opportunity for my family and career. (Adam Goldstein, MEd, PhD)

After graduating from college, I planned to pursue a career in law and quickly became disenchanted with the thought of legal practice. I explored careers in higher education and grew interested in the possibility of becoming a dean of students. I sought my master's degree in college student affairs while finishing law school. Following graduation, I worked part-time in student conduct at a large, state institution while studying for the bar exam. Thereafter, I obtained my first full-time professional role as the director of student conduct and assessment at a small, religious, liberal arts institution.

Recognizing that I springboarded into a directorship and remained interested in pursuing a deanship, I intentionally used my time as a director to become knowledgeable about and to gain experience in other functional areas outside of student conduct and the CARE [campus assessment response and education] (behavioral concerns) team. Six years later, I was promoted internally following a national search for the next assistant vice provost for student formation and campus life and dean of students. My decision to become a dean of students was made in consultation with my family, as I recognized that the responsibilities of the position would affect them in different ways. Serving in the associate vice provost and dean of students' role is more demanding on my time, which is challenging as I balance raising a family that includes three young children. Yet, it is deeply rewarding to challenge and support students while contributing to a vibrant, transformative learning process within a campus community that supports me personally and professionally. (Lauren Scott Rivera, JD, MEd)

While each of our backgrounds is unique, we recognize the roads we have taken are not the only ones that lead people to these challenging but fulfilling positions. In this chapter, we will explore the diverse pathways taken by sitting deans in hopes of providing valuable insights for those aspiring to serve as deans of students.

A Survey of Deans of Students

We are familiar with a body of literature about preparing to serve as a senior student affairs officer (SSAO), and some organizational structures have the dean of students serving as the SSAO. However, there is little written about the ever-changing dean role and the various pathways to becoming a dean. For this reason, we designed a brief survey to explore the various professional and educational pathways to the dean of students' position. Recognizing that each pathway is unique in what it offers to those preparing for the deanship, we also asked questions to confirm the most pressing issues faced by deans today. By understanding these issues, we are better able to consider how the various pathways prepare individuals to navigate the most pressing challenges.

In May 2018, we invited 412 sitting deans of students who are members of NASPA–Student Affairs Administrators in Higher Education to complete an electronic survey. We received responses from 57.3% (n = 236) of our colleagues. Approximately 58% reported working full-time in higher education for 11 to 20 years before securing their first dean of students' position, while 29% of respondents noted 10 or fewer years of full-time work in the field before assuming their first deanship. The remaining 13% indicated they worked for 21 or more years before transitioning into their first dean role. While we hoped to garner insights from deans of students at different types of institutions, nearly 92% of respondents worked at 4-year institutions. Accordingly, our survey results are not necessarily reflective of the pathways and experiences of deans at 2-year colleges. Of those deans who worked at 4-year schools, 57% were at private, not-for-profit institutions; 40% were at public institutions; and 3% were at private, for-profit institutions.

In addition to gleaning data from the aforementioned survey, this chapter includes our personal reflections, as well as information gathered through conversations with consultants who work for three professional search firms that support colleges and universities in searching for deans of students when vacancies arise. The chapter is divided into four sections, the first of which explores various educational pathways to the dean of students' role. The second part considers the experiences gained prior to moving into the deanship, while the third section examines the most pressing issues that deans of students are facing today and how the development of key competencies can assist in navigating these challenges. Finally, the chapter concludes with advice from sitting deans that will help aspiring deans in preparing for, assuming, and sustaining themselves in the dean of students' role.

Exploring Educational Pathways to the Deanship

Since the late twentieth century when colleges and universities combined the dean of men's and dean of women's positions to create a dean of students' position, the expectations and responsibilities of deans have expanded and become more complex (Hevel, 2016). Early deans of men and women focused on student discipline and housing, while the responsibilities of today's deans of students are much broader and more intricate. Given this development, the knowledge base and skill set required to successfully navigate the complexities of the role have grown. Knowledge acquisition occurs in part through pursuit of formal degrees within the academy. However, the importance of experiential learning and ongoing professional development cannot be overstated and will be explored in this chapter. With the professionalization of the student affairs field, most who seek a career in student affairs attain a master's degree in higher education, student affairs administration, college student personnel, or a closely related field. Furthermore, people who aspire to serve as deans of students often continue their formal education through pursuit of doctoral, professional, or other advanced degrees. In fact, according to one search consultant, pursuit of a doctoral degree by aspiring deans has become more common over the past decade, which reflects that student affairs has continued to evolve into an established profession that requires formalized training and expertise. Given the varied educational backgrounds of current deans of students, those who aspire to deanships should consider the diverse roads to the role, as well as the benefits and drawbacks of each pathway on their personal and professional lives.

Master's Degrees

Many student affairs professionals who focus their work within specific functional areas such as residence life, student activities, or student conduct hold a master's degree in student affairs administration, administrative leadership in higher education, counseling, or a related field. Some of these individuals later transition to a dean of students' position without pursuing additional degrees. All sitting deans who responded to our survey had at least a master's degree, and 32% reported that the master's degree was their highest degree completed. These individuals are employed at various types of 2- and 4-year public and private institutions across the United States. Although their fields of study vary, 63% of responding deans for whom a master's degree was their highest degree completed stated that their degree was in student affairs administration, administrative leadership in higher education, or a similar program. Another 17% indicated that their degree was in counseling. Other fields of study included, but were not limited to, public administration, business, and the humanities.

Individuals who ascend to the dean of students' role with their highest degree being a master's degree are more likely to do so through internal promotion. Nearly 60% of respondents for whom a master's degree was their highest degree were internally promoted after holding an associate dean, assistant dean, director, or similar position at their current institution. In these instances, the work ethic and strengths of the individual are known within the community, and the person's command of institutional culture coupled with existing relationships can make navigating the transition more manageable. The importance of relationship building cannot be overstated for those in the dean of students' role, as well as those who hope for an internal promotion to the position. "The dean of students' position requires relationship building at all levels of the institution from students through senior leadership," noted one sitting dean. Another offered the following advice: "Assume nothing. Pick up the phone and make the call or walk over and give a visit." Strong relationships can provide a foothold for those transitioning into the deanship. Institutions that might prefer a dean have a terminal degree may be more willing to overlook this credential when there is a known and trusted internal candidate with demonstrated leadership potential.

While internal promotion is the most common path to the deanship for people whose highest degree obtained is a master's degree, approximately 15% of such respondents reported serving in the dean of students' role at a different institution immediately prior to assuming their current deanship. According to search consultants, most institutions searching for a dean of students strongly prefer or require that the successful candidate have a terminal degree. However, one can surmise that colleges and universities might prefer to hire an individual who has a proven capacity to navigate the complexities of the dean of students' role through demonstrated experience regardless of whether he or she has a terminal degree.

In sum, with more than one-third of responding deans confirming their highest degree was a master's degree, this remains a viable formal educational pathway to the deanship. However, one key drawback involves the perception by others within the institution, particularly faculty, that an individual with a master's degree does not possess the same level of expertise as campus colleagues who hold terminal degrees. There is no shortage of master's–level student affairs professionals who have extensive experience serving in positions up to and including the directorship of large, complex functional areas. These colleagues have demonstrated the ability to navigate the most common challenges facing deans. However, these professionals may struggle to make progress in their quest to obtain a dean of students' role. When this occurs, it may be because of the emphasis placed by many institutions on the terminal degree credential for senior administrators.

Terminal Degrees

While it is possible to ascend to a deanship with a master's degree, search firms that assist colleges and universities in their efforts to identify their next dean of students note that a doctoral or other terminal degree is generally required or at least preferred by employers. However, this credential must be accompanied by the necessary experience in the field. For this reason, aspiring deans should strongly consider pursuit of a terminal degree. Nearly 66% of sitting deans who responded to our survey reported having a terminal degree, and an additional 2% confirmed they were working on their terminal degree. Like 2 of the contributors to this chapter, most deans of students who hold a terminal degree have a doctor of philosophy (PhD) or doctor of education (EdD) degree focused on student affairs, higher education, or a closely related course of study. Data confirmed this, as 80% of respondents who completed doctoral or other terminal degrees studied student affairs administration, administrative leadership in higher education, or a similar field. Counseling was the next most popular field of study among those with terminal degrees, though just 5% took this path. Other fields of study included, but were not limited to, psychology and law.

Student affairs professionals who decide to pursue a doctoral degree in education often grapple with whether the PhD or EdD is the better path. In general, the PhD degree is competency based, research intensive, and intended for those seeking to become scholars in their field of study. Many PhD students work part-time as research or teaching assistants, which gives them experience while helping to cover the costs of their degree. Between the coursework and a dissertation, the PhD can take longer to complete than the EdD and may be viewed as a more prestigious credential particularly by faculty at some institutions. In addition, people who aspire to teach at colleges and universities, which includes some deans of students, may lean toward the PhD, as it is the more common road for faculty members. Adam decided to pursue his PhD in student affairs administration after working full-time in student affairs at two institutions. In the following, Adam outlined his decision to pursue a PhD on his road to the deanship:

> After seven years of work, five years of marriage, and the arrival of our first child, I decided to pursue my PhD. Our daughter was born prematurely, which prompted deep introspection about our future. My wife stopped working to care for our daughter, and we decided that I would pursue my doctorate full-time for several reasons. First, if I was going to make my career in higher education, I believed I should have the highest degree the industry offered. Second, given my learning style and work ethic, I could not envision working full-time, studying part-time, and being present for my family. I needed to prioritize my studies over work to get the full benefit of my final degree. Third, if I studied full-time, I would likely have an assistantship that paid for the degree though offered very little take-home pay. We knew we would need to live very lean for the next few years, and we thought it would be best to do so while our child was young.

Finally, I wanted the doctoral experience to springboard me to the next stage of my career. This meant seeking an assistantship outside my area of expertise, something that would serve as a bridge to other professional areas and responsibilities. Studying part-time would not provide me the opportunity to earn my degree and gain experience in areas I believed essential for my career growth.

While the PhD has the advantage of being more widely respected by faculty, many aspiring higher education professionals who seek terminal degrees pursue an EdD. This is because it is practice focused and can typically be completed on a part-time basis. The EdD is structured around coursework and is less research intensive than the PhD. Professionals who pursue the EdD often do so while simultaneously gaining experience through full-time employment. Just as people considering faculty work tend to be more interested in the more theoretical and research-focused PhD degree, people who seek administrative positions are often drawn to the EdD, which is geared toward preparing practitioners to navigate challenges that educational administrators encounter. Jacob's road to the deanship involved pursuit of his EdD immediately upon completion of his master's degree:

> I was fortunate to apply for and receive the Bill and Melinda Gates Millennium Scholarship, which provided funding for my education. I received this during the first year of my master's program, and upon learning that the funding would continue through the doctorate, I jumped at the opportunity to continue my studies. In my case, I pursued a master's degree in higher education and student affairs administration and subsequently an EdD in educational leadership and policy studies. The funding allowed me to pursue my doctorate full-time, and the EdD was the highest degree offered at my institution at the time. Two important factors informed my decision to stay at the institution where I received my master's degree. First, I had tremendous professional opportunities and support from the dean of students' office. Second, I was fortunate to have a doctoral adviser who attained the status of full professor and was highly invested in helping me achieve my dream of finishing my terminal degree. These are the primary reasons why I persisted, and I continue to be grateful for having had these opportunities.

Although they are the most common degrees for deans of students, the PhD and EdD degrees are not the only terminal degrees that aspiring deans should consider. A handful of survey respondents indicated that they pursued a legal education, thereby achieving the terminal degree of juris doctor (JD). This degree, sometimes referred to as a doctor of jurisprudence, is a professional doctorate degree. Compared to other terminal degrees, the JD is a road less traveled by those in student affairs, but an increasing number of people within higher education hold this degree. It is a pathway worth consideration given the changing landscape of higher education particularly with respect to legal and compliance issues and the impact of these changes on the deanship.

Over the past decade, the dean of students' role has grown more complex in part because of significant events in the world. The 2007 tragedy at Virginia Tech, for example, prompted increased attention to campus safety, mental health, and behavioral intervention, and the 2014 unrest in Ferguson, Missouri, spurred more conversation on campuses about race relations, activism, social justice, and campus safety. The time deans spend understanding and making decisions aligned with laws and regulations has ballooned in an effort to ensure legal compliance on a broad range of issues such as mental health, sexual violence, freedom of speech and expression, and hazing. Many deans of students, when asked to offer advice, suggest that aspiring deans gain expertise in legal compliance by participating in conferences or otherwise engage in training focused on law and policy. With this advice coming from so many, it is more appropriate now than ever before for aspiring deans to consider the less traveled JD route. Of course, a law degree is most advantageous when coupled with professional experience in various functional areas within student affairs and pairs well with a master's degree in student affairs, higher education, or a similar field of study. Lauren's formal educational pathway to her deanship involved the simultaneous pursuit of a JD and master's degree in college student affairs:

> When I graduated from college, I entered law school in hopes of pursuing a career through which I could help others via family law and child advocacy; I had never considered working in higher education. Two months into law school, I struggled to see myself as a practicing lawyer and grew worried that I chose the wrong career. After talking with family and reflecting on my passions, I explored new opportunities and contemplated whether I should quit law school to work toward a career in higher education. As part of my discernment process, I met with several senior student affairs officers and deans of students to learn about their work and career paths. Most pursued doctoral degrees in higher education administration or a similar field. To my surprise, each person I spoke with strongly encouraged me to return to law school because of the increasingly complex legal landscape of colleges and universities. The insights of sitting deans are what prompted me to return to law school and to work with the administration to develop a dual-degree program that ultimately allowed me to pursue a legal education while simultaneously completing a master's degree in college student

affairs. These conversations are also what initially piqued my interest in helping others by serving as a dean of students.

Ensuring Breadth and Depth: Reflecting on Experiential Learning Prior to the Deanship

In reflecting on what it takes to succeed in the deanship, one professional search consultant stressed that an aspiring dean is greatly disadvantaged when moving into the dean of students' role if the person has not had previous experience with making decisions that have broad institutional impact. Such decisions often relate to students engaged in high-risk behaviors, thorny legal issues, or highly politicized matters that involve the president or other senior campus leaders. This speaks to the importance of having a depth of professional experiences that exposes one to handling institutional vulnerability or, better put, what keeps the senior student affairs officer or president awake at night. Beyond the requisite formal education, the preparation needed to serve as a dean of students today can be parsed into the following areas: (a) gaining practical professional experiences, (b) reflecting on one's motivation to serve as a dean, and (c) establishing a community of supportive mentors.

Gaining Practical Professional Experience

In exploring the practical professional experiences of sitting deans, our survey asked respondents about the areas in student affairs for which they had responsibility immediately prior to assuming their dean of students' role. Sitting deans reported that the most common areas of responsibility just prior to their deanship were as follows:

- Student conduct (behavioral): 50%
- Campus activities: 47%
- CARE team or behavioral intervention team (BIT): 47%
- Student conduct (academic): 42%
- On-campus housing: 37%

Managing entities like student conduct or a CARE team, whose role is to provide support to students struggling with medical issues, mental health, or other significant personal circumstances, certainly prepares individuals for the crisis management responsibilities often within the dean's purview. As one respondent shared, "There is no neat road to the dean of students' position. Not many of us have checked all of the boxes prior to assuming the role."

The aforementioned data do not prescribe a pathway to the dean of students' role, yet it is important to note that intentionally seeking experiences that require an individual to work collaboratively with academic affairs, finance, legal, and student affairs colleagues offers an opportunity to develop knowledge and skills that will set one up to succeed as a dean. In sum, both our personal experiences and the data gathered from sitting deans confirm the importance of having both a breadth and depth of experience. This, coupled with formal education, prepares one to carry out the day-to-day responsibilities of the dean of students.

Reflecting on Motivation to Serve as Dean: The Personal Dimension

In reflecting on the different roads to our deanships, we could not ignore the personal dimension in the pathway of preparation. The demands on this position affect not only the person serving in the role but also the people closest to this person. As Jacob navigated his career, one that included two deanships and a stint as an SSAO, he found it beneficial to reflect on the following questions:

- What motivates me to pursue this role?
- What kind of institution and mission would be the best fit for me?
- What demographic of students do I feel called to serve?
- What aspects of the role may deplete or give me energy?
- Am I (and are my loved ones) willing to commit to being on call, responding to campus issues on nights and weekends, and being available for consultation at any time should the community need my perspective?

Similar to Jacob, Lauren found it helpful to reflect deeply on her identity, her motivation, her calling to serve as a dean of students, and the unique support she would need as a working mother before deciding to pursue her first deanship:

After five years as the director of student conduct and assessment at an institution some four hours from my extended family, I began searching for assistant dean and dean of students' positions in the metropolitan area where I was raised. Family was always an incredible support and source of encouragement for me, and I could not fathom a journey toward the deanship without them nearby. Although married and with one young child, I remained steadfast in my desire to serve college students by assisting them in navigating challenges that affect their success. Unfortunately, positions in the area on which I focused my search were few and far between. This prompted me to consider how my calling to pursue a deanship meshed with my desire to return home.

At 39 weeks pregnant with my second child and after much discernment, I applied to serve as the associate vice provost and dean of students at the institution where I held my directorship, despite its distance from home. One factor that contributed to my decision was the plethora of support I felt as a woman committed to raising a family while working in a demanding role. I recognized that, if hired, I would be working for and with a number of working mothers—people who understood the importance of working from home when needed by a sick child, people who offered to help with a sick child while I attended a critical meeting, and people who supported the integration of work and family. After I was promoted into the deanship, my appreciation for my "village" and the family-friendly mission of the institution grew. I continue to be grateful for these colleagues who remind me of what matters most, who encourage me to strive for excellence personally and professionally, and who support me as I continually work to better balance and integrate my identities as a wife, a mother to three beautiful children, and a tireless student advocate and dean of students.

For Adam, a family crisis helped him see the impact a caring dean of students can have on students and families in distress. This resulted in a strong sense of purpose, which motivates him in the performance of his duties as a dean:

My first experience with a dean of students came unexpectedly. During my senior year in college, my cousin was severely injured in a near-fatal car accident and taken by helicopter to a hospital near my school. I rushed to meet my aunt and uncle and stood next to them as the dean of students from his college arrived to support our family. I remember her caring presence and offer of support and how much it meant to my family that she came to the hospital herself. It was a powerful interaction that I vividly remember more than 25 years later. At the time, I had no idea that my life journey would one day lead me to be a dean, yet I think of her every time I interact with a student or family in crisis.

Establishing a Community of Mentors

One last and important dimension to consider is the importance of identifying your personal metrics of career success and to seek out mentors who can provide a listening ear and provide sage feedback as you discern your pathway. It is not advisable to seek the job title as an emblem of success, as this is unlikely to sustain a person in the role. Rather, it is important to reflect deeply on why you are called to serve a college or university community in this capacity. The following excerpt, offered by Jacob, illustrates how reflection coupled with the use of mentors can be beneficial in making career decisions:

> David Nestor, dean of students at the University of Vermont, is a mentor and someone I call for career advice. Over the years, he has often highlighted for me how institutional fit contributes to one's professional satisfaction and helps to lift oneself up when an institution does not behave in alignment with its stated values. He has also reminded me of the importance of serving in a community that speaks to the core of who I am even when all public metrics of success (i.e., title, salary, status, etc.) may cause me to pause and, as a result, consider turning down the volume on my own calling.
>
> In my career, I have had the privilege of serving as a dean of students, an SSAO, and now again as the dean of students. In each role, I have benefited from excellent mentorship and support. Each position has also refined the focus of my calling. In my first dean of students' role, I served excellent students, some of whom came from middle- and upper-class backgrounds. As an SSAO serving a similar demographic, I found myself reflecting deeply on whether I was intended to serve students who may not have access to financial and social capital in the same way. The more I reflected on my upbringing as a Chicano from a bilingual home who grew up in a working-class environment, the more I felt called to serve larger numbers of students of color and first-generation college students. Currently in my second deanship, I have found the place where I can serve students who are pushed to the margins and where access continues to be a value of the institution's senior leadership. While it is uncomfortable at times, I think it is critical to deeply consider whether your current role meets your personal and professional goals, is congruent with your values, and intuitively feels right to you.

In review, gaining both a depth and a breadth of practical professional experiences, reflecting on one's motivation to serve as a dean of students, and developing a mentoring community are key ingredients in preparing to pursue a deanship. The following account, offered by Jacob, highlights the three dimensions of preparation covered in this section and sets the stage for the discussion that follows regarding the myriad pressing issues facing today's deans of students:

> I began my career in housing and residence life and in multicultural affairs. I also had the fortune to serve as a special assistant to the dean of students for three years while I worked on my doctoral degree. As a special assistant,

I took meeting minutes, scheduled appointments, and participated as an active member of the director's group in the division of student affairs. This exposed me to a broad conversation about student affairs and gave me insight into the day-to-day challenges directors faced. To say this was eye-opening is an understatement. Thankfully, my more seasoned colleagues were generous and grace filled as they answered my questions about their respective functional areas and listened intently as I voiced perspective.

This experience gave me insight into the galvanizing role of a central administrative office for a division and reinforced my aspiration to serve as a dean or vice president. Last, I learned the importance of being engaged in a professional association such as NASPA, American College Personnel Association (ACPA), Association of Student Conduct Administration (ASCA), and others. This involvement gave me opportunities to network and build relationships that I am fortunate to have. I have a circle of friends and mentors whom I trust and can call at any time for advice and a listening ear. In closing, I will share what one mentor said to me: "Jake, the association is there for you and needs to take care of you." I have found this to be true repeatedly as I have faced serious challenges in each of my roles. I cannot overstate the importance of maintaining a close group of mentors; they will lift you up when you are down and celebrate your successes.

Preparing to Be a Dean: What Roads Should I Travel?

Compared to 10 years ago, crisis management and response, sexual assault and prevention, and other competencies dealing with campus climate and culture (i.e., protests, activism, free speech and expression) are all very important experiences to have. (Search firm professional on changes in dean of students' search processes)

The best way for aspiring deans to prepare for the role is to understand the landscape navigated by current deans. The roles and responsibilities of a dean of students can vary greatly depending on the administrative structure and scope of responsibilities and institutional size and type. However, our experience, and the results of survey respondents, revealed several common elements important for aspiring deans to understand. These include the ability to grapple with complex issues and concerns, the confidence to work through ambiguity, the capacity to balance strong character with humility, a desire to learn, the ability to manage conflict alongside the personal and professional demands of the role, the willingness to develop and sustain strong relationships, and the skill to supervise staff and departments.

The search firm professionals we spoke with identified a broad range of knowledge, skills, and experiences aspiring deans need to demonstrate to show their readiness for the role. One noted that candidates for the position should be able to explain, in detail, the things they are already doing to help a community navigate the complex issues of the day. Another emphasized the detailed responses candidates will need to provide in their interviews. One search agent shared, "They want to know what you are currently doing to reduce risk for your community specific to the vulnerabilities of student life. Theoretical and conceptual responses will no longer suffice." Crisis management, sexual assault and prevention, hazing prevention, campus climate, student activism, free speech and expression, and compliance with mandates, policies, and procedures were all identified as areas of importance. On the skills and experiences that benefit aspiring deans, one sitting dean stated, "I find that people who have worked in the area of conduct and related topics advance to dean positions more easily because they have dealt with pressure, difficult decisions, and learned to be very clear with students and parents around difficult topics."

When sitting deans were asked about the top health, wellness, and safety issues they currently manage, 98% identified mental health concerns, 70% indicated sexual assault, and 48% identified suicide prevention specifically, a subset of mental health. One sitting dean advised, "Today's dean calls for someone who can carefully and compassionately manage the many mental health issues that present themselves on campus, particularly for those living in the residence hall." These issues can occur at any time, can be upsetting to many, and can take an emotional toll on those not trained or experienced managing these issues. A search firm professional said, "These jobs are intense and 24/7, and you should have a real discussion with yourself if that is a lifestyle you are ready and prepared to take on."

When sitting deans were asked about the top administrative issues they currently manage, 64% stated campus crises, 62% indicated compliance and regulatory requirements, and 57% highlighted diminishing resources. One search firm professional said, "The knowledge base [required of a dean] is so much larger now, there are a lot of things they need to know that shapes how they respond on behalf of the university. . . . [It is] a much more technical role, the policy issues are more sophisticated today . . . the language needs to be more precise. . . . Deans need to consider, 'Will a decision stand up in court?'" Though the following advice didn't make the top-three list, one sitting dean shared, "Be prepared to handle more supervision and human resource issues than student affairs work." Though this may not be true for all, experience with personnel management was raised by many sitting deans in the advice they provided to those aspiring to the role.

Of the top campus culture issues deans currently manage, 88% of the sitting deans surveyed indicated diversity, equity, and inclusion; 50% identified campus safety; and 48% stated the changing student demographic. These issues are often complex and require the dean to demonstrate compassion, confidence, and fortitude while remaining focused how the issues affect the student community. As one search firm professional emphasized, "It is important for an aspiring [dean of students] to get into a part of the university that has some high-stakes, fast-paced, unpredictable elements to it."

Of the top student learning and success issues current deans manage, 75% indicated student persistence, 58% stated assessment and accountability, and 54% said cocurricular learning outcomes. In the current era of regulation, compliance, and accountability, deans of students will need to be adept at setting measurable goals that demonstrate institutional requirements are being met, prevention efforts are decreasing harmful outcomes, and programs and initiatives are contributing to student learning. This is challenging work, and aspiring deans would do well to gain experience with assessment and reporting prior to taking on the role. One way to gain this experience is by offering to help your current dean with assessment efforts. Many deans are balancing their time between response to individual and community crises and strategic planning and assessment; any dean of students would likely appreciate the offer of assistance.

Conclusion

In this chapter, we explored various formal educational pathways to the dean of students' role, considered the professional experiences that current deans of students had immediately prior to assuming their deanship, and reflected on how formal education and professional experience prepared sitting deans for their roles. Thereafter, we identified the most pressing issues facing deans of students today and reviewed advice for those aspiring to the deanship as shared by sitting deans and search firm professionals. Having navigated our way to this dynamic and challenging role, we advise aspiring deans of students to reflect on their professional strengths and weaknesses and begin acquiring the skills and experiences that will inform their decisions at the crossroads they meet prior to a deanship. Each of us carries within ourselves great accomplishments, significant challenges, and everything in between that we have encountered along our pathways to the dean of students' role. We carry these experiences—some of which date back to childhood and college—within us each day as we seek to advocate for, serve, challenge, and support students in their quest to persist and thrive in higher education. We believe it is important to know your story and the important parts of you that compel you toward the role. In addition to thinking how to prepare for the role, set aside time to consider how your experiences will inform your service as a dean of students.

Finally, while we have pearls of wisdom to offer those considering in the future or currently serving in a deanship, in an effort to be inclusive of more voices, we distilled the following advice from the data collected in the survey referenced throughout this chapter:

- *Develop a professional network and identify trusted mentors.* Developing a professional network and strong mentors helps in transitioning into a deanship and succeeding in the role. To "find your [professional] village," join one or more professional organizations. Getting involved helps you meet people and share your knowledge. Go to conferences and institutes with the intention of networking and forming relationships. You learn from other's successes and challenges. Seek out mentors, people who offer sage advice and with whom you can be vulnerable as you learn and grow. As one dean noted, "I didn't really know the power of mentors until I had colleagues I could trust to share my experiences with and could look at my situations objectively because they've been there before. You always want folks in your corner to tell you when you're right . . . and to tell you when you're wrong."

- *Engage in ongoing professional development.* Keeping current in an evolving field can be difficult, but it is critical to success for deans of students. Eight sitting deans stressed the importance of investing in your ongoing professional development to continue growing while remaining up-to-date on issues and challenges in higher education. Although budgets for professional development can be tight, look for opportunities that help you sharpen your skills or dive deep into a functional area. National and regional conferences, institutes, coursework, and webinars are wonderful for professional development. However, carving out time in an otherwise busy schedule to read *The Chronicle of Higher Education, Inside Higher Ed,* and other key publications is equally as important.

- *Prepare to navigate increasingly complex laws and policies.* Most deans of students do not follow an educational pathway that involves pursuit of a law degree. However, as many sitting deans shared in their advice, it has become imperative for deans of students to have a command of law and policy and be comfortable reviewing regulations and case law. Even deans who benefit from easy access to their institution's general counsel realize that the frequency with which they are faced with legal compliance matters demands that they are competent in this area. A good primer is Peter F. Lake's (2011) *Foundations of Higher Education Law and Policy*. For ongoing development in this area, consider conferences, certificate programs, and publications. Some of these include the NASPA Certificate Program in Student Affairs Law and Policy, the National Conference of Law and Higher Education (Stetson University), the Legal Issues in Higher Education Conference (University of Vermont), and information shared by the National Association of College and University Attorneys (NACUA).

- *Keep a pulse on and nurture campus relationships.* The dean of students' role is different from others in that deans need to develop and maintain relationships with a broad range of campus constituents within and outside of student affairs. As a dean, you need to call on others for assistance sometimes in the midst of a crisis. You need to build partnerships and collaborations to accomplish goals. You also need to liaise with administrators, faculty, and staff in support of students. Most important, deans must maintain open lines of communication with students for whom they serve as lead advocate, have close relationships with student leaders, and understand the experiences of students from marginalized backgrounds. Do not just rely on e-mail. Take the time to call people, visit colleagues' offices, enjoy coffee or a meal together, and listen to the stories of students. As one sitting dean noted when stressing the importance of relationships, they "are the currency of the [campus] kingdom."
- *Understand the emotional pitch of students.* The dean of students, as the lead student advocate, is often called on to convey the pulse of the student body even more so than the vice president for student affairs. One sitting dean articulated that a key difference in the roles of the vice president and dean of students relates to

> the institutional strategic lens and the student-facing, personal support dimension. For the vice president, strategy and the student affairs agenda is the work in the abstract without daily regard to the emotional pitch of the campus. It is the role of the dean of students to pay attention to and prioritize this pitch.

Indeed, when many in a community shy away from complex, volatile campus culture issues, a dean's orientation must be to move toward them. To prepare for the deanship, aspiring deans should practice leaning into challenge.

Authors' Note

We wish to extend a heartfelt thanks to NASPA for the assistance as we constructed our dean of students' survey. In addition, we are grateful for the search consultants from Isaacson Miller, Spelman and Johnson, and Witt Kieffer, who offered their insights with us so that we could share their unique perspectives with readers.

References

Frost, R. (1916). *Mountain interval.* New York, NY: Henry Holt and Company.
Hevel, M. S. (2016). Toward a history of student affairs: A synthesis of research, 1996–2015. *Journal of College Student Development, 57*(7), 844–862.
Lake, P. F. (2011). *Foundations of higher education law and policy: Basic legal rules, concepts, and principles for student affairs.* Washington, DC: NASPA.

3

THE JUGGLING ACT

Navigating Competing and Complicated Demands

Shadia Sachedina and Anna Gonzalez

O n a rainy winter day a few years ago, one of the contributors to this chapter received a call from her campus police. A student from her institution had jumped from a building and died instantly. Of all the things that the then first-year dean of students thought she would have to deal with that day, or even that year, this type of tragedy and crisis was the furthest from her mind. As she reflected on this incident, a well-attended session at a national conference came to mind. The topic at that session was about becoming a dean of students and everything about this seemingly grand role. When it came to question-and-answer time, one of the panelists (a dean of students who was well-known in the field) was asked to share a perspective on the most difficult moment as dean. The response was "to be the person who has to call a parent about the death of their child." What had lured many of the attendees to this session was an attraction to the impressive stature associated with being a dean of students. And, yet, not realized are the unique and often competing roles inherent in the position itself. While the title seems to have a ring of authority and even accomplishment, it carries with it a weight that only those who have actually held the position can truly understand.

There is a complicated juggling act that is endemic to the role of the dean of students. This act involves a seemingly never-ending string of navigating competing and complicated demands. Do you remember that plate spinner featured on *The Ed Sullivan Show*? That is the life of a dean of students. This chapter will focus on how to thrive in the role, without dropping any plates, all while navigating the competing demands that confront you. Our collective experiences from various institutions ranging from large research universities to medium-size universities to small liberal arts colleges serve as the foundation for this chapter. The chapter itself is divided into three main sections. We first focus on what the dean of students manages, followed by how a dean is able to juggle various demands. Our chapter concludes with some recommendations to our colleagues on ways to be successful in this role. We hope that after reading this chapter, you will find that while the journey as a dean of students can be fraught with unexpected pitfalls and many hard knocks, it has also led to some of the most fulfilling accomplishments in our careers.

What Do You Manage as the Dean of Students?

According to Komives and Woodard (2003), "the Dean of Students carries the burden of helping students while establishing and enforcing both community standards and institutional standards at the same time" (p. 346). This position often means that the dean has multiple and many times competing constituents that will expect time, attention, and support. In addition to this, the dean of students must be able to respond to a wider range of constituents from families to faculty to community members as it relates to a diverse array of issues that arise on our campuses (Komives & Woodard, 2003). Depending on the type of institution, areas that this role oversees may include judicial affairs, cultural centers, student activities, residence life, health and counseling services, public safety, and even athletics.

Like all positions, the dean of students' role comes with an outlined set of responsibilities that are clearly marked on the job posting. However, unlike with other positions, what deans end up handling exists more and more in the section denoted as "other duties as assigned." That nebulous statement encapsulates all aspects of the role that we were unaware of or rather did not comprehend as being something that would come under the dean of students' purview. This could include anything from setting up a food pantry on campus to creating a program to address the homeless student population. It could involve overseeing the logistics of commencement and at the same time working with the narcotics division of the local police department to assist in investigating a major drug problem in the student community. The constant stream of demands comes from all sides, including students, faculty, staff, direct reports vice presidents, the provost, and the president.

A standard question asked by younger professionals interested in dean of students' work is "What is a typical day like as dean?" There is no typical day. Figure 3.1 provides an illustration of a day in the life of a dean of students. We thought a visual representation would help drive the point home.

Figure 3.1. What is a typical day like as dean?

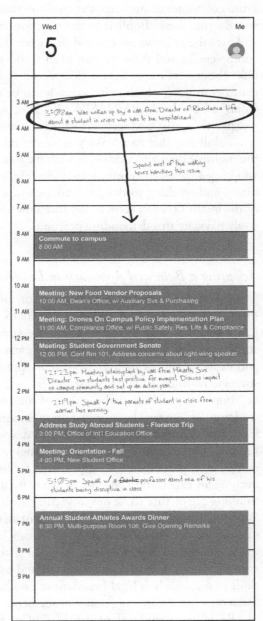

What is a Typical Day Like as Dean?
There is no typical day.

Recall you started your day at 3:00 a.m. and this day was different from yesterday and will be different from tomorrow and the day after that.

How Do You Manage as the Dean of Students?

From colleagues to students, the question that often comes to us is "How do you do your job?" Implicit in the question is the concept of competencies, and over the years we have found that what the question really means is what competencies and skills do you need to do your job? Often, the literature talks about needing to have a clear vision and a detailed set of objectives to get to your goal, which many consider to be the why or purpose of the job. Informed by the ACPA/NASPA (2015) competencies and our own collective practices, this next section focuses on ways to develop your competencies (your skill set) that can make you successful when you attempt to manage the multiple demands that come with the role. In this section we discuss how adopting a balanced approach to leadership, building cross-campus communities, and working to develop and sustain a network of colleagues outside of the institution can serve as key instruments in getting you set up to effectively navigate this demanding position.

Adopting a Balanced Approach to Leadership

The challenges we face in higher education are numerous and run the gamut from student access and retention efforts to the development and maintenance of sustainable programs that have strong track records in improving student success rates. These challenges demand creative, innovative thinking and expect a caliber of leadership that approaches the work in a balanced strategic manner. To be effective leaders, we, as deans of students, can't rely on simply responding to the caring of the emotional and physical needs of students. We are now being relied on to respond to student needs on a "meta" level, one that demands our learning to develop innovative ways to increase funding, understand the constantly changing world of governmental policy compliance, participate in campus-wide facilities planning, and so on. It has become an expectation that when we plan and make decisions that we are thinking big picture while not forgetting the lived experience of our students. While many graduate programs in student affairs and higher education focus on student development and the psychosocial behavior of adults, the dramatic changes in higher education mean that there is a greater need to also ensure that one gains the philosophical and hands-on approach to leadership skills in areas such as legal foundations and human resources with a specific focus on supervision and fiscal management.

Based on a study of successful CEOs, Kaplan and Sorensen's (2007) brief article in *Harvard Business Review* argued that hard skills are much more important than soft skills. We are not suggesting that deans of students necessarily emulate CEOs. In fact, we do not think that one set of skills is better than the other. Nye (2008), Harvard emeritus dean and professor and author of multiple books on power and leadership, wrote, "Smart leaders need both *soft and hard power skills*" (p. 147) to lead. In recognition of this, we believe that future and current deans of students need to understand that having a varied and diverse leadership skill set is one of the keys to success in this role. Although it is hard to have an equal amount of talent for both hard skills and soft skills, it is important we strive for balanced leadership abilities so that we can use them when needed as part of our skill set.

As an example, many deans of students oversee housing and student unions. In this vein, their concern cannot be only programming and community building. Rather, overseeing these areas means that deans must have an even greater need to demonstrate their understanding of the complexities and cost-benefit analysis of expanding opportunities for the creation of more revenue-generating options for the institution. The overall budget of their division, and even the university, depends on how these auxiliaries meet or even improve their fiscal health within the limits of what they can provide to students. Case in point, Varlotta and Jones's (2010) edited collection titled *Student Affairs Budgeting and Financial Management in the Midst of Financial Crisis* features articles written by SSAOs who collectively enumerate the importance of being known as a leader in financial budgeting in higher education. As a dean of students, you must not only understand and select appropriate budget strategies but also have the necessary skills to effectively communicate these plans to your various stakeholders. Thus, your leadership style requires some adaptability in the way you choose to approach this particular issue. You will need to adopt a collaborative and persuasive approach when working with constituents like those in the student government who might be voting members on your auxiliary board and instrumental in getting a vote passed for your division's budget. At the same time, you will need to shift your style when addressing the board of trustees as you work to convince them that using these extra dollars for a program initiative coordinated and implemented within your division is the right direction for the institution. Adopting this strategic and balanced approach in how you lead will have a long-term positive impact on the day-to-day management and oversight of key areas that fall under your purview.

Building Cross-Campus Communities

As this chapter posits, deans of students juggle multiple and sometimes competing tasks at the same time. One can do all of these things only if there is support from colleagues within and external to the division. Managing multiple demands can be easier if you develop strong relationships with individuals throughout your campus. The temptation to always be in charge of a situation whether it is something that involves a sense of fun or is a crisis is not sustainable over any period of time. Instead, we can experience success by building a community of support with other divisions and involving them in helping us solve the crisis du jour. The action of building positive, collegial relationships carries long-term rewards toward creating an environment of trust within the institution and building our own reputations as being strong collaborators invested in the success of the student body.

Collaboration within higher education is not always a natural act. In fact, one of the things that gets in the way of our doing our jobs effectively and often creates additional work is the existence of silos within the institution. As an instrument in creating pathways to student success, a dean of students who can successfully build bridges between student affairs and academic affairs can be a powerful benefit to the institution. Take, for example, a first-year experience program created by student affairs in collaboration with academic affairs to help retain undergraduate students at an institution. As student affairs educators, we understand that learning occurs in and out of the classroom. What better way to be seen as a collaborator than to help lead a campus focused on student success as a fundamental outcome of higher education (Banta & Kuh, 2010)?

As deans of students, we have established committees and task forces made up of individuals from various departments who are not always from the division of student affairs and, in fact, do not report up to us. This is not merely a strategy to have buy-in for an initiative that may be seen as controversial or difficult to implement. Rather, the act of collaborating and working with those not from student affairs not only allows us to gain a different perspective on how students are engaged with other departments and vice versa but also impresses on us ways to improve on the way we conduct business and serve students within our own areas. Overall, the collaborative partnerships we create with others can not only serve the needs of students but also help alleviate some of our burdens by opening up opportunities to share the load with campus partners who might be more of an expert on the project at hand. As an example, a student who may be showing high stress and causing serious disruption in the residence halls may initially seem like one who someone within student affairs (e.g., student conduct or dean of students) may have to manage. However, on further evaluation, the student CARE team, which includes individuals from academic affairs and other areas, finds that the student is experiencing severe stress due to a rather large and extremely demanding academic workload. A trusting and collaborative relationship between academic and student affairs colleagues can ensure that information is shared between both areas. The more qualified support staff, in this case those from the academic advising office, serve as the initial contact to ensure that the student gets the proper support and assistance.

Building and Sustaining a Network Outside of Your Institution

The final portion of this section discusses the importance of establishing and maintaining a network of supportive colleagues outside of your institution. Colleagues from across the country who make up this support system serve as trusted advisers, mentors, and peers whom you can lean on, laugh with, cry with, or simply commiserate with about an issue at hand or simply the job itself. You can start building these networks as early as graduate school or as recently as meeting someone at the last conference you attended. In addition to serving as sounding boards, these networks also serve as informants on the latest trends in our field, provide data including best practice efforts at similar institutions, and give us another perspective about how to address a situation or provide a service to students. It stands to reason that having a supportive network outside of our institution can be an invaluable resource for our continued growth and success and play a significant role in building our skill set.

Let us now turn our attention to using these important skills and applying them to the task of managing competing and complicated demands.

Understanding the Institution and Institutional Culture

As leaders within the organization, deans of students succeed in balancing competing interests and completing multiple tasks by understanding how things work within the structural organization of the institution. Understanding both the culture and the dominant organizational frame or frames within which an institution operates can give a dean of students significant agency with both the day-to-day and long-term strategic planning that is a part of the job.

As an example, a week for deans can look like the following:

- Presenting to the board of trustees on retention
- Addressing a student's death
- Giving a speech honoring students who received scholarships
- Meeting with a parent who has concerns about a staff member you supervise
- Being a judge at a student-run talent show

- Meeting with the Student Government Association to discuss its plans to bring a controversial speaker to campus
- Working with your director of health to manage the quarantine of two students diagnosed with mumps (and concurrently coordinating campus communiqué about this matter)
- Attending a residence life master plan meeting with your facilities, administration, and finance teams to discuss a major renovation and overhaul of the residential facilities on your campus

Important to your success when managing these competing commitments is your ability to understand organizational frameworks and the institution's culture. This way you have a better understanding of the ways in which priorities are set and communicated at your institution. Despite its importance, many leaders either forget or worse dismiss the culture of their institution, often because it is not something that one could easily see, touch, or define. Described as the invisible tapestry within an organization, institutional culture unearths the hidden codes about the inner workings of a university and how one can get things done. These persistent patterns of norms, practices, values, and beliefs often drive what we can and cannot accomplish and can be a major roadblock if we choose not to understand how to work within or around it (Kuh & Whitt, 1988). Missteps can happen in the most unexpected ways. For instance, imagine that a new dean of students, you would like to establish a task force that would look into a policy and practice regarding the option for students to have their preferred name on their college ID, class attendance roster, and other locales. You invite individuals from departments across the campus and include faculty, staff, and students to ensure that you have an inclusive and collaborative process. Everything appears to be going smoothly, and your meeting invitations have been accepted by the pertinent people who would be involved with this process. Suddenly you receive a summons from the provost, who wishes to discuss with you the way you chose to determine the committee membership. You find out that while not officially noted anywhere, the practice of inviting individuals to be members on a committee must begin with a request to division heads to identify available personnel from their units who would be able to sit on the committee. This practice, which may appear hierarchal, has been a part of the institutional culture for years and has been perceived by the campus as a strategic control of human resource because the institution has seen a significant shortage in the workforce, along with an increase in demand for participation in task forces and committees. Thus, to ensure that nothing gets in the way of the creation of much needed services or policies, it is important to be aware of the norms and practices at your institution.

We mentioned earlier about the importance of understanding the organizational framework within which you, as the dean of students, should learn to operate. Bolman and Deal's (2013) work on organizational theory and change management is a valuable resource in contributing to understanding frameworks. Their work discusses four major frames that inform practitioners on how universities operate. Knowing which of the frames your institution most often operates within can allow you to navigate and solve short-term and long-term job-related challenges.

The structural frame relies on the premise that there are organizational charts with defined division of labor within the team. Furthermore, this frame works within the understanding that decisions are made with a rational mind-set and organized coordination and in line with established goals and objectives. The human resource frame focuses on the human or individual within the organization. It focuses on fit and emphasizes motivation, training, commitment, and socialization. The political frame is the one that Bolman and Deal (2013) found to be most downplayed by women and educators. Despite some negative connotation on the word *political*, leaders who use this frame have become experts at understanding relationships based on power dynamics and are often adept at developing coalitions and allies to support their initiatives and ideas. Finally, the symbolic frame is highly dependent on rituals, meanings, ceremonies, purpose, and emotions for the functioning of the organization. Of the four frames, this fourth one looks at valuing what is expressed and felt rather than what is actually produced.

To see these frames in action, let us look at an example. As a dean of students you are alerted by your residence life director about two male fraternity pledges with multiple physical injuries who have been hospitalized in serious condition. The fraternity being held responsible has a long-standing legacy of service at the institution. Their alumni are very involved with the college; two of them serve on the college's board of trustees and are major donors. In addition, the college provost is a member of this fraternity. This issue can be viewed through all four frameworks:

1. *Structural:* There is an organized process within which this issue should be addressed. The college has a well-defined student code of conduct, which includes a zero-tolerance policy when handling issues that involve hazing.
2. *Human resource:* Your role as the dean of students is kicked into high gear here. You need to operate from a space of compassion and student advocate for all parties. Your role involves maintaining an objective demeanor

as you engage with not only the students and their families but also their lawyers, the Panhellenic student council, the campus newspaper, the president, and other senior administration of the college.

3. *Political:* The long-standing legacy of this fraternity, its alumni involvement, and its ties to members of the institution that include the president and the provost of the college makes this issue extremely political. There are power dynamics here that could very well supplant your efforts to resolve this issue through a structural lens.

4. *Symbolic:* Again, the long-standing legacy of this fraternity at the institution, its high-profile membership, and the strong financial support it has given to the college goes back decades. As an important detail, the student union is named after one of its members.

Essential to the way you address this situation is your understanding that you will need to operate within several frames at once. You cannot handle this issue through a single frame, and entwined within this entire issue is the institutional culture and the way it operates at moments like these. Organizational frames can coexist in one institution or even within your own division of student affairs. In addition, individuals within the same office may lean toward one frame over another. You as the dean of students may value the structural frame and create what you see as a very orderly flowchart on how to deal with a crisis. In contrast, your president and provost may both operate within the political frame and have their own sense and understanding of how a crisis should be handled and who should be involved in the decision-making process. There is no right or wrong answer to this issue. Rather, it is important to be able to discern the types of frames your institution operates within and figure out how best to make sure that your style can complement it. Also essential is your ability to communicate why your working frame should be the dominant one to use in a particular situation.

Finally, while institutional culture and operating frameworks are already embedded within an institution by the time you arrive at your campus, it is reassuring to know that deans of students can be influencers, and over time your influence will affect the way things operate.

Understanding When Something Is a Crisis and When It Is Not

It is important to understand the definition of a crisis in order to truly determine if something, in fact, rises to that level. There are various definitions of crisis available within the literature. Pearson and Clair (1998) conducted a broad study on crisis management processes and provided this comprehensive definition of a *crisis*:

> A low-probability, high impact situation that is perceived by critical stakeholders to threaten the viability of the organization and that is subjectively experienced by these individuals as personally and socially threatening. . . . During the crisis, decision-making is pressed by perceived time constraints, and colored by cognitive limitations. (p. 66)

When asked to define this term, fellow deans of students provided a wide range of responses, which included definitions such as "a crisis is immediate threat to student safety or mental and physical state." Another response stated, "A crisis is an unplanned, unpredictable situation that could create great financial and/or emotional stress to an institution and its constituents (i.e., students, faculty, and staff), as well as its short- and long-term reputation."

Too much of the job is unpredictable, and to the extent possible, we need structure so that in the event of a crisis, we have a process already in place that can provide us with the scaffolding we need to develop a response plan. Much of the success that comes with navigating the competing demands of serving as a dean of students is learning to recognize a crisis. Most situations are not actually a crisis, but we are programmed to react reflexively to the way the problem is presented. If we work with an attitude that sees problems as something to be afraid of, then we are more apt to respond to them very much like how a child reacts to a boogie monster under the bed. We tend to overreact, and this can result in the problem snowballing unnecessarily. There is also the danger of underreacting to a problem. For instance, we have neglected to notice that a student who has been found sleeping overnight in a campus lounge on multiple occasions is the same student who has been acting out in an academic classroom and disrupting the environment. Our lack of attention to these incidents results in a mounting crisis that escalates into a major conduct issue. However, to an earlier point, if we view crises as part of our everyday job, then chances are good that we will respond in a matter that will allow us to manage the situation from a sense of calmness and presence. Ultimately, in a crisis the only real power we have is in how we choose to approach the situation. Therefore, our response should be shaped not by the perceived chaotic nature of the problem but from an inward place of confidence and purpose that adds credence to the reasoning behind why we were hired to serve as a dean of students. Qualities that make you an effective dean of students are what you need to help you resolve a crisis. Johnson (2018) noted, "The leadership competencies required for successful crisis leadership are same as those required for successful leadership in daily organizational life. It is just that the circumstances are sometimes profoundly different" (p. 16). In other words, be yourself, but just get better at it.

Crises can be categorized in different ways. Johnson (2018) described a crisis as either "incident" driven or "issues" driven. For the purposes of this book, incident-driven crises would be something like a residence hall fire, a major hurricane and evacuation effort, a bomb threat, or a campus shooter. An issues-driven crisis is more of a slow burner type, the one where you can see it coming and, if you are mindful enough, can set up some potential solutions in place to mitigate its effects. For instance, a poorly managed student activities office responsible for the handling of student activity fees could potentially lead to a disaster during auditing season. Also, alternative spring break trips that are poorly supervised and not chaperoned appropriately are a liability issue just waiting to happen. Last, the lack of a campus behavioral intervention team could result in disjointed efforts in managing care and providing support to students in need. All of these issues-driven crises are the types that can be proactively addressed without their morphing into a major career-ending crisis.

On the other hand, James Haggerty (2017) in *Chief Crisis Officer* scoffed at the notion of categorizing a crisis in any other way but a crisis. His theory is that attempting to label a crisis as an incident or an issue could result in downplaying of the matter at hand, and this could result in a major problem that would be difficult to come back from. "From a risk management standpoint," he wrote, "an incident or issue should be managed with the same seriousness and care as a crisis, since it may just be a crisis that hasn't exploded yet" (p. 5). Like Johnson (2018), Haggerty also delineated a crisis into two main types: exploding and unfolding. Like Johnson's incident-driven crisis, an exploding crisis is the type that happens quickly and must be responded to right away. The issues-driven crisis is Haggerty's definition of the unfolding type.

How should we navigate a crisis whether it is exploding (incident driven) or unfolding (issues driven)? The two most valuable assets you can have when faced with a crisis are *time* and *space* (Johnson, 2018). Work at slowing down the momentum of the situation as much as you can so that you can buy yourself time to thoughtfully explore best possible solutions. Set up space for you to think, ideally with a support network standing by. Most important, whether a crisis is issues driven or incident driven, how you choose to respond is dependent on one very important question: Are you prepared?

The best way to be prepared is to have a crisis response plan in place that encompasses any and all types of issues that can arise. Haggerty (2017) discussed the necessity of having a working plan always on tap to be able to address a crisis no matter how big or small it might be. His strategy calls for the development of ACT (assess, create, train), a plan that can easily be translated for the higher education environment.

To assess (step one), we identify categories of crisis and the key constituents whom you would work with to handle each type. These crises can be categorized into five specific areas:

1. *Health and safety:* Examples of health and safety crises include a mumps outbreak, a major flood in a residence hall, food poisoning reported from a multicultural festival sponsored by a student club during Latino Heritage month, a distressed student with behavioral concerns acting out in the classroom, and your office receiving reports of students who are homeless and/or disclosing a lack of funding available for purchase of food.
2. *Technology:* Examples of technology crises include Blackboard going down during finals week or some enterprising students developing an app that is able to hack into the campus course registration system and wreak havoc on the registration process.
3. *Financial:* You are alerted to possible embezzlement of student activity fees estimated at several hundred thousand dollars.
4. *Personnel:* Staff members file a complaint against one of your department directors claiming discrimination.
5. *Political:* A student government protest against a controversial speaker results in campus sit-ins and organized marches to the president's office.

It is important to note that the list of scenarios is far from exhaustive, yet the categories they fall into can be fairly well contained. This can then help to create a crisis management plan that could be applied with success. Once you have developed a list of possible scenarios that you might be dealing with, you should create (step two) what Haggerty (2017) called a road map. This consists of an outlined plan of action for each issue and the team that you can bring together immediately to help you navigate the issue. In every one of these possible scenarios, it is important that you have an identified team to work with in handling the situations. Because the crises are so varied in type, having a preidentified set of people for each category gives you a better ability to control and manage the issue. Thus, no matter what the issue might be and however outlandish it appears, the right team by your side can help you manage successfully. The key players on each team might be different for each scenario. For instance, health and safety issues might involve campus environmental health and safety, the health and wellness director, and public safety; technology issues would require your information technology colleagues; and still yet, financial issues would require your coordination with the finance and budget office. The possible configurations of collaborators depending on the context of the crisis are never ending.

Within each category the response would also involve multiple layers and would vary depending on the kind of situation. For instance, food poisoning from a multicultural festival might involve not only the intervention of your health center but also dialogue led by the multicultural office with students who blame their illness on "that Spanish food." A student in distress exhibiting behavioral concerns in the classroom would need the intervention of something like a campus CARE team or behavioral intervention team, an already preestablished crisis response group that deals specifically with students in distress. Because the CARE team is composed of constituents across campus (academic advising, residence life, faculty representatives from the academic schools, health services, etc.), the student could be supported in multiple ways (e.g., through immediate assistance via the counseling center or assistance through the academic advising office with the student's stressful course load). The key to handling these multiple types of crises is to be able to punt to your team members and trust in their judgment in working with you to handle the crisis du jour. In some scenarios, you would do well to include your communications office to help with the potential public relations issues that can arise from a crisis. Last, training (step three) is vital. A successful crisis management plan will require having a team that is confident and able to tackle an issue head on with a clear sense of what needs to be done. This can be done through ongoing development exercises devoted exclusively to learning how to navigate these "what if" scenarios. Identifying training dates that are placed on people's calendars months in advance can help provide structure and establish an expectation that clearly demonstrates the importance of the issue.

Developing a Strong Team

One of the keys to effective management of competing and complicated demands is the presence of a highly functioning, self-efficacious team of colleagues who stand strongly by your side and help you manage the daily onslaught of demands and requests that stream your way.

Assuming that part of your role as the dean of students involves supervision of various functional areas within student affairs, it becomes a priority for you to invest a significant portion of your time in the development of a trusting and collaborative relationship with your direct reports. Building trust with your direct reports takes time and a keen sense of self-awareness.

Learn to Understand Your Direct Reports

An initial step in developing your relationships is assessing each of your direct reports' professional competencies as student affairs professionals. The *ACPA/NASPA Professional Competencies Rubrics* (ACPA/NASPA, 2015) can be used to develop a self-assessment tool that individuals can fill out prior to an initial meeting with you. While some of your direct reports may be subject matter experts in their particular functional areas, for instance, health, counseling, or disability services, they may not be very proficient in successfully transitioning their expertise into the broader higher education environment. Using the *ACPA/NASPA Professional Competencies Rubrics* as a way to gauge their understanding of their expertise in relation to the university environment is a useful way to begin engaging in intentional and strategic problem-solving using the benchmarks clearly outlined in these competency rubrics.

Another useful tool to use to access the talent potential of these professionals and improve their morale and professional engagement in the field of student affairs is Gallup's Strengths Assessment (Clifton & Harter, 2003). By using this tool, individuals can become self-aware of their strengths and develop their acceptance of the unique combination of their talents. Gallup's strengths-based approach is built on the philosophy of positive psychology, which focuses on what people do well rather than homing in on their weaknesses (Clifton & Harter, 2003). This approach encourages individuals to develop their identities through increased awareness of self thus leading to improving their innate talents, skills, and abilities. Adopting a strengths-based approach to individual development has a positive impact on employee engagement, productivity, well-being, and confidence, among other outcomes (Clifton & Harter, 2003; Hodges & Clifton, 2004). In fact, Gallup research has shown that employees who use their strengths daily are six times more likely to be engaged at work (Sorenson, 2014).

Strengths-based coaching can be used in conjunction with the *ACPA/NASPA Professional Competencies Rubrics* (ACPA/NASPA, 2015). For instance, you can create a self-assessment tool using the rubric as a guide. Staff can be asked to complete the self-assessment as part of an evaluative process. Then, using results from the Gallup Strengths Assessment (Clifton & Harter, 2003) as a foundation, you can engage in some thoughtful and intentional conversations with your direct reports. The rubric serves as a useful guide, helping staff see where they might fall on the spectrum of foundational, intermediate, or advanced. More important, the rubric–strengths combination gives the evaluation added weight and keeps it focused, specific, and positive. It can be an uplifting and empowering experience to work with people in actualizing their true potential. More often than not, the conversations turn to their challenges and concerns in navigating their work environment and working with their supervisors and those they supervise. Using the Strengths Assessment as the language to help guide those conversations is particularly helpful. The Strengths Assessment will not tell you what to do, but the tool provides useful guidance in helping you see how to apply your talents productively. This means that whether challenged by difficult projects or working with recalcitrant staff, the Strengths Assessment provides you with the tools to coach your team to use their talents to succeed.

Develop the Emotional Intelligence of Your Team

Understanding the strengths of each of your direct reports can be used strategically in building the emotional intelligence (EI) of your team. In their article "Building the Emotional Intelligence of Groups," Druskat and Wolff (2001) discussed critical elements to group effectiveness, specifically "trust among members, a sense of group identity, and a sense of group efficacy" (p. 82). Effectively developing these three conditions relies on the establishment of group norms or standards of behavior where individual members must not only possess individual EI but also be able to work successfully as a group to regulate each other's emotional behavior and the emotions of constituents outside of their immediate circle (Druskat & Wolff, 2001). It stands to reason that familiarity with the Strengths Assessment can serve as a useful tool in helping team members build their EI, as they would become better able to handle conflict and hold each other accountable in a caring and trusting manner.

Regardless of how emotionally intelligent your team might be, conflicts do arise, and this can get in the way of helping you effectively get the job done. It is during these times that conflict can be kept constructive and focused on the issue at hand as opposed to devolving into a negative interpersonal battle of wills (Eisenhardt, Kahwajy, and Bourgeois (1997). For instance, let us say members of your team are grappling with a request submitted by the student government to bring in a controversial speaker to campus. While some members of the group are comfortable with this request for various reasons, others are outraged and express hurt and bewilderment at the supporters of this program. In these instances, the best way to resolve and move forward is to home in on the issue at hand and step away from the personal debate that can arise. In the article

"How Management Teams Can Have a Good Fight," Eisenhardt, Kahwajy, and Bourgeois (1997) suggested several tactics to address conflict-ridden issues:

- *Focus on the facts:* What have other institutions done when dealing with controversial speakers on their campus? Assign someone on the team to do some research and make necessary phone calls to student affairs colleagues to gain some insight on this issue.
- *Multiply the alternatives:* When deciding what to do, consider a variety of alternatives, even those you don't support. For instance, in this particular scenario, contemplate bringing in multiple controversial speakers; perhaps host a weeklong series of controversial speakers on campus. No doubt, this could well be a public relations nightmare and a major security risk. The point is that suggesting multiple alternatives could help "diffuse conflict [around the team table], and prevent teams from polarizing around just two possibilities" (Eisenhardt et al., 1997, p. 77).
- *Create common goals:* In a concerted attempt to bring the team to consensus, work toward a common purpose or purposes. In this instance, it could be to protect First Amendment rights and the safety and security of the campus community and to support the student voice.
- *Use humor:* It is so crucial to find moments of laughter in the work that we do. Finding the space to use good-natured, appropriate humor could help ease the tension in the moment.
- *Balance the power structure:* Make space for every voice to be heard and valued, especially during times of conflict. This may require you to keep track of how often you are speaking versus listening as an example to your team.
- *Seek consensus with qualification:* While the ultimate goal is to create consensus, in some cases this does not happen. In those instances, the person with the most senior authority would make the decision. In such a circumstance, the process for how the decision was made, which includes ensuring that all voices were heard, will directly affect the degree to which your team buys in to the outcome.

Create Multiple Groups With a Variety of Skill Sets

For you to optimize your ability to manage competing priorities, it is critical that you are effective in setting up multiple groups to help you navigate your priorities. These priorities are varied, and it stands to reason that you create intentional groups whose skills are specifically geared toward producing the best results in each of those areas. For instance, some of the groups you could create would handle areas that involve student orientation, students in crisis, sexual violence education, establishing community standards, and student health and wellness. In all these instances, these established groups are engaged in addressing various aspects of student affairs that affect the student experience.

Setting up these groups must be done with an eye toward what you are looking to achieve. To that end, you should differentiate between these groups as either teams or working groups. In "The Discipline of Teams," Katzenbach and Smith (1993) discussed the role of working groups as different from that of a team. A "working group's performance is a function of what its members do as individuals," while a "team's performance includes both individual results and what [they] call 'collective work-products'" (p. 2). Very often, we assume that a group of people working closely together is a team; however, working groups are not necessarily a team. Teams tend to band together around a common purpose, their product is very often a sum of their collective parts, and they function through a process of mutual accountability. Working groups, on the other hand, band around the institutional mission and operate through individual accountability. Their effectiveness is measured "indirectly by its influence on others" (Katzenbach & Smith, 1993). For instance, representatives from campus constituents like residence life, student life, academic affairs, communications and marketing, facilities, public safety, and health and wellness could be brought together as a working group to address student orientation. Constituents would be responsible within their individual functional unit to contribute toward the institutional goal for creating an engaged student experience vis-à-vis orientation. Its effectiveness would be measured by overall student satisfaction of the orientation experience.

However, a group created to address student behavioral concerns would be set up as a team; for instance, a CARE team or a behavioral intervention team. In this instance, the mission of the team would be one that bands around a common purpose. The success of the team depends on its collective work together to problem solve around issues involving students experiencing distress. The effectiveness of the team would be measured by assessing its collective impact on handling students in crisis.

It is impossible to expect the dean of students to head up every one of these teams and/or working groups. Instead, strategically work with your direct reports and identify key members of areas to lead up some of these groups. Create an accountability system where you expect daily or weekly reports to stay abreast of current situations. It is important that you have set up some clear communication guidelines with your team members so that they know what situations require your immediate attention and what can wait till your biweekly individual meeting.

Conclusion

We began this chapter with a story about a student who died by suicide. That incident set into motion a number of institutional responses that included not only delving into understanding exactly why this transpired but also maintaining close and consistent communications with the student's family, the senior membership of the institution, and members of the student community; engaging with the student's professors; and organizing a campus-wide memorial. At the forefront in the coordination of these efforts was the dean of students. There was no time to step back and strategically think through every step. It was game time, where you had to trust in the fact that your experience in the field had prepared you for moments like these. To aid in getting you ready for that moment of pivotal leadership, this chapter covered the depth and breadth of what a dean of students has to manage. We provided you with some helpful tools and strategies on how you can learn to manage (juggle) the constant influx of demands. It is an irrefutable fact that as a profession, student affairs has grown beyond an advisory role to students. Our students and their needs have become more complex, and it seems as though we encounter a new issue or challenge on a daily basis. A decade ago, we would never have thought that our job would have included drafting a policy on emotional support animals on our campus or a campus death protocol, ensuring that students understand our policy related to the use of social media and stalking, or coming up with language that explains the new ban on plastic straws. Indeed, colleges and universities work with students who are the products of the world that we have become. These students bear the joys and burdens of the ever-changing, more complex society that is wrapped up in 24-hour news, Instagram, drones, the possibility of self-driving cars, and Amazon's "1-click" and "Alexa."

We end this chapter by reminding our readers that despite the juggling act we face, despite the hurried pace at which we often live, and despite the many crisis moments that may at times swallow us, we value what we have learned in our careers as deans of students. This position has allowed us to provide transformative experiences for generations of students, many of whom continue to positively affect their own corner of the world. Our work rewards us with the privilege to work with future leaders of our world. With each challenge or new issue that might arise comes the potential to be innovative. Each story we encounter comes with the potential for creating bigger and better opportunities for students, a better life, and a better world. And at the end of it all, we learn how to be better jugglers and role models for future deans of students.

To assist you in your juggling act and managing all that there is in being a dean of students, we summarize our primary recommendations, couched in the hypothetical situation with which we opened this chapter:

- *Master essential competencies of student affairs:* By adopting a balanced approach to leadership, you are able to successfully engage with campus community members who range from students to faculty to senior-level administration. You have built strong cross-campus relationships that help you navigate the investigation of the incident and the coordination of campus-wide initiatives that need to take place following this suicide. Your network of supportive student affairs colleagues outside of the institution provide you with necessary perspective and important things to be mindful of based on their past experiences.
- *Understand your institution's culture:* Your ability to accurately discern the frameworks within which your institution functions and your in-depth understanding of the institutional culture help you proactively engage on the political front with senior leadership, provide a space for students to come together and commemorate their classmate (human resource and symbolic), and adhere to the established campus death protocol that you developed for your institution (structural).
- *Understand when something is a crisis and when it is not:* Sadly, we know from experience that given enough time in the role, you will develop a wide skill set in defining and managing crisis. However, never miss an opportunity to help your colleagues develop into strong partners in such eventualities.
- *Build a strong team:* The time and effort you have expended in the creation of a team that is committed to student success set you up to be able to appropriately delegate and trust in the members' abilities to help you navigate this challenging issue.

References

ACPA/NASPA. (2015). *ACPA/NASPA professional competencies rubrics.* Retrieved from https://www.naspa.org/images/uploads/main/ACPA_NASPA_Professional_Competency_Rubrics_Full.pdf

Banta, T. W., & Kuh, G. D. (2010). A missing link in assessment: Collaboration between academic and student affairs professionals. *Change: The Magazine of Higher Learning, 30*(2), 40–46.

Bolman, L., & Deal, T. (2013). *Reframing organizations: Artistry, choice, and leadership*. San Francisco, CA: Jossey-Bass.

Clifton, D. O., & Harter, J. K. (2003). Investing in strengths. In *Positive organizational scholarship: Foundations of a new discipline* (pp. 111–121). San Francisco, CA: Berrett-Koehler.

Druskat, V. U., & Wolff, S. B. (2001). Building the emotional intelligence of groups. *Harvard Business Review*. Retrieved from https://hbr.org/2001/03/building-the-emotional-intelligence-of-groups Retrieved from.

Eisenhardt, K. M., Kahwajy, J. L., & Bourgeois, L. J.,III. (1997). How management teams can have a good fight. *Harvard business review*, 75(4), 77–85.

Haggerty, J. F. (2017). *Chief crisis officer: Structure and leadership for effective communications response*. Chicago, IL: ABA Publishing.

Hodges, T. D., & Clifton, D. O. (2004). Strengths-based development in practice. In P. A. Linley & S. Joseph (Eds.), *Positive psychology in practice* (pp. 256–268). Hoboken, NJ: John Wiley & Sons.

Johnson, T. (2018). *Crisis leadership: How to lead in times of crisis, threat and uncertainty*. New York, NY: Bloomsbury.

Kaplan, S., & Sorensen, M. (2007). In leadership, "hard" skills trump "soft" skills. Retrieved from https://hbr.org/2007/12/in-leadership-hard-skills-trum

Katzenbach, J. R., & Smith, D. K. (1993). The discipline of teams. Retrieved from https://hbr.org/1993/03/the-discipline-of-teams-2

Komives, S., & Woodard, D., Jr. (2003). *Student services: A handbook for the profession* (4th ed.). San Francisco, CA: Jossey-Bass.

Kuh, G. D., & Whitt, E. (1988). *The invisible tapestry: Culture in American colleges and universities*. San Francisco, CA: Jossey-Bass.

Nye, J. (2008). *The powers to lead*. New York, NY: Oxford University Press.

Pearson, C. M., & Clair, J. A. (1998). Reframing crisis management. *Academy of Management Review*, 23(1), 59–76.

Sorenson, S. (2014). How employees' strengths make your company stronger. Retrieved from https://news.gallup.com/businessjournal/167462/employees-strengths-company-stronger.aspx

Varlotta, L., & Jones, B. (2010). *Student affairs budgeting and financial management in the midst of fiscal crisis*. San Francisco, CA: Jossey-Bass.

4

STUDENT CONCERNS, ADVOCACY, SUPPORT . . . AND YOU!

Denise Balfour Simpson and Akirah J. Bradley

It's my job to advocate for students. Our campus community needs to know about our students' needs so that they can engage in the process of creating initiatives designed to meet these needs. Advocacy includes telling the stories of students' experiences, empowering students to share their own stories, and identifying ways to support student success. We cannot ignore these needs if we want our students to succeed.—Carolyn Golz, associate vice president and dean of students, University of New Orleans

The dean of students' role is a complex position that has continued to evolve over time. Regardless of university type, the dean of students' leadership and expertise remains constant and most imperative amidst multifaceted student issues, especially working in "gray areas" where there are no clear-cut answers. A dean of students must be able to create a path even when one is not paved, institute protocols, and establish structure as new challenges emerge. Perceived as a "doer," the dean of students is called on for strategy development; situation management; dialogue with students; and, at times, repair of harms to and restoration of trust within the campus community.

The positionality of the dean of students' role is to balance being a student advocate and serving the institution in a holistic manner. Circumstances that find their way to the dean of students' desk often need immediate attention and can have a huge impact on an individual student or all students. The dean of students must have good instincts, high levels of political acumen, and a thorough understanding of campus culture. This professional is a bridge from the student body to senior campus leadership and must maintain a pulse on current issues facing students and college campuses. This chapter will highlight the ongoing trends of issues affecting students and the role the dean of students plays to address these concerns. Free speech, hate speech, and student activism; bias response; behavioral intervention teams (BITs); student conduct; Title IX; and fiscal challenges related to students' unmet needs will be discussed.

When Free Speech, Hate Speech, and Student Activism Collide

Higher education institutions have seen the demand of free speech throughout history. The free speech movement began in 1964 at the University of California, Berkeley, which emerged as a free speech hub and led an unparalleled trend of student activism that continues today. Issues spanning the globe motivated some of the largest student protests and demonstrations, such as the civil rights movement, opposition to the Vietnam War, and urging of divestment of apartheid in South Africa (Cohen, 1985).

More recently, higher education institutions have seen an upsurge in student activism. The Educational Advisory Board (2017) stated, "The current wave of student activism is expected to intensify in coming years, due to changing demographics on campus and increasingly high expectations from students" (p. 4). Students have led and taken part in demonstrations regarding Title IX, the Black Lives Matter movement, sanctuary campuses, and gun violence and in opposition to conservative speakers on campus. The current tension between free speech and hate speech has caused uproar on college campuses, resulting in increased student activism.

> On the University of Colorado, Boulder's campus, it has been my experience that the dean of students plays an integral role in the support of student engagement, advocacy, and agency in students' education journey. I have found many of my dean of students' colleagues at both private and public universities are involved in continued and evolving conversations centered on free speech and freedom of expression and assembly. A few of my colleagues and I organize phone check-in meetings once a month, and free speech and protest are a consistent topic of discussion. (Akirah J. Bradley, associate vice chancellor, former dean of students, University of Colorado, Boulder)

The First Amendment protects the freedom of religion, expression, speech, press, assembly, and petition of the government. The right of expression, speech, inviting the press, and assembly have converged simultaneously with student demonstrations on college campuses. The United States Courts (2018) website helps outline examples of protected speech, which include the following:

- Not to speak (specifically, the right not to salute the flag): *West Virginia Board of Education v. Barnette,* 319 U.S. 624 (1943)
- Of students to wear black armbands to school to protest a war ("students do not shed their constitutional rights at the schoolhouse gate"): *Tinker v. Des Moines,* 393 U.S. 503 (1969)
- To use certain offensive words and phrases to convey political messages: *Cohen v. California,* 403 U.S. 15 (1971)
- To engage in symbolic speech (e.g., burning the flag in protest): *Texas v. Johnson,* 491 U.S. 397 (1989); *United States v. Eichman,* 496 U.S. 310 (1990)

These examples reference where the courts ruled in favor of protected speech. It is essential that those in the dean of students' position understand the difference in practical application to free speech based on institutional type and according to federal and state legislation. Public universities are legally bound to uphold the First Amendment and protect free speech. Private institutions operate under agreements between the university and the student; agreements are based on each private university's policy (Silverglate, French, & Lukianoff, 2012).

The Foundation for Individual Rights in Education (Foundation for Individual Rights in Education, 2017) posited,

> Although acceptance of federal funding does confer some obligations upon private colleges (such as compliance with federal anti-discrimination laws), compliance with the First Amendment is not one of them. This does not mean, however, students and faculty at private schools are not entitled to free speech. In fact, most private universities explicitly promise freedom of speech and academic freedom. (pp. 8–9)

Moreover, some states have implemented legislation to provide further guidance for private and religious universities. For instance, California Education Code §94367 (1992), also known as the Leonard Law, stated,

> No private postsecondary educational institution shall make or enforce a rule subjecting a student to disciplinary sanctions solely on the basis of conduct that is speech or other communication that, when engaged in outside the campus or facility of a private postsecondary institution, is protected from governmental restriction by the First Amendment to the United

States Constitution or Section 2 of Article I of the California Constitution.
. . . This section does not apply to a private postsecondary educational
institution that is controlled by a religious organization, to the extent that
the application of this section would not be consistent with the religious
tenets of the organization.

Higher education institutions have grappled for decades with finding ways to
manage when free speech is also hate speech. For instance, Stanford University
implemented a speech code barring bigoted speech, prohibiting insults based on
race and sex. This incident led to *Corry* (1995) and the Superior Court of Santa
Clara County to rule Stanford's speech code violated the freedom of speech
rights guaranteed to its students under California's Leonard Law (Associated
Press, 1995). How far can universities go to respond to hateful speech that
causes unrest on campus without violating freedom of expression? In Stanford's
case, not very far. Both private and public institutions in California must follow
California state law, and private colleges and universities may not have the same
flexibility of private institutions in other states.

In addition, several states have begun to ban free speech zones on college
campuses. For example, Colorado Senate Bill (SB17-062) (2017) passed ban-
ning free speech zones on college campuses in Colorado and giving students
freedom of speech and expression anywhere on campus with the caveat to not
disrupt previously scheduled or reserved activities. Students who believe their
speech is restricted by SB17-062 can now bring court action. SB17-062 also
noted,

A public institution shall not impose restrictions on the time, place, and
manner of student speech unless such restrictions are reasonable, justified
without reference to the speech's content, are narrowly tailored to serve a
significant government interest, and leave open ample alternative channels
for communication of the information or message.

This bill is a shift for some colleges and universities in Colorado. Colleges
and universities in Colorado with free speech zones in their policies must
change to align with this new legislation.

Other states may soon adopt similar legislation to limit a college campus'
ability to impose time, place, and manner. This legislation comes at a time when
the collision of free speech and hate speech has fostered conditions for strife
and division within the student body, faculty, and administrators. One article
stated, "The term *hate speech* is frequently applied as a synonym for speech that
is racist, sexist, homophobic, or similarly pejorative" (Silverglate et al., 2012,
p. 108, emphasis added). The American Civil Liberties Union (n.d.) stated,

How much we value the right of free speech is put to its severest test when the speaker is someone we disagree with most. Speech that deeply offends our morality or is hostile to our way of life warrants the same constitutional protection as other speech.

These quotations sum up the struggle seen across the nation that offensive and hostile speech is protected under the law. On college campuses, there is an expectation from some students of protecting their emotional safety, and by law colleges and universities cannot shut down speech because it is offensive.

One consideration for deans of students when responding to free speech incidents is to review campus policies and protocols that address discrimination and harassment based on protected identities, which generally include race, national origin, pregnancy, sex, age, disability, religion, sexual orientation, gender identity, gender expression, and veteran status. Bias-motivated incidents are reported to an administrative office or a team within the university to prevent, educate about, and respond to situations where a university community member is being targeted with harassment or discrimination based on a protected class status. Bias incidents can be challenging to address, because often there is not a specific respondent involved. An example of this is a flier with hateful language hung up in the student union; this may be reported to a bias response team to address. For bias or hate speech to rise to a level where speech is not protected, behaviors rising to immediate threat or harassment should exist, which can be a difficult threshold to meet. Often university administrators lean toward restorative justice—formal practices that seek to address harmful behaviors and develop a culture of inclusive decision-making, active accountability, repairing harm, and restoring trust (Karp, 2013) or other creative ways to resolve bias-based incidents.

A major challenge on college campuses is balancing the rights and protection of individuals who may be severely affected by offensive speech and the creation of space that protects all speech no matter how harmful it is. Each person has protection of First Amendment rights, and that same protection gives people the freedom to engage in behavior and say words that cause pain and trauma and potentially create a campus environment of unrest. Consequently, deans of students respond when free speech imposes emotional harm to their campus communities and are often expected to act swiftly and repair any damage immediately. One duty of deans of students is to create an atmosphere of critical thinking and exchange of different perspectives and ideologies, while also making decisions about what should or should not be allowed at a university event. Striking this balance may also lead to an inherent catch-22 when federal, state, and local policies; institutional politics; and student perspectives and expectations are at play. Nothing paints this picture better than the uptick in controversial speakers and White nationalist rallies that are sparking news headlines:

- "'Grave Concerns' Over Controversial Middlebury Speaker" (Johnson, 2017)
- "Conservative Groups Sue Berkeley Over Ann Coulter Cancellation" (Fuller, 2017)
- "Texas A&M Cancels 9/11 White Nationalist Rally Amid Safety Concerns" (Ayala, 2017)
- "Inside the U. of Virginia's Response to a Chaotic White-Supremacist Rally" (Stripling, 2017)

Controversial speakers on college campuses have been widely covered in news stories over the past year, and institutions have had varying opinions about responses to and results of managing perceived harmful speech. Some institutions have canceled speakers, whereas others felt obligated to host the speakers. In these cases, private colleges and universities have more latitude to cancel events depending on their written policies, in contrast to public universities, where legal action can be taken for violating freedom of speech if they decide to cancel the event for reasons that may be a violation of federal or state law. Thus, free speech, hate speech, and student activism coalesce, along with the intensity of media scrutiny, as campus leaders come together to manage the competing campus and community expectations. As conservative speakers continue to make their way on campuses, some students who are not in favor of the message organize demonstrations and exercise their free speech against the message of the speaker.

Milo Yiannopoulos's college tour is an example of where free speech, hate speech, and student activism collided. His stop at the University of California, Berkeley, received much attention as the campus community and local nonuniversity affiliates expressed themselves through protest that became violent (Quintana, 2018). Consequently, the university canceled the event, which resulted in a lawsuit. In addition, an incredibly scary incident ensued at the University of Washington, as detailed in the following vignette:

On the night of January 20, 2017, Milo was scheduled to take the stage at the University of Washington. It was a very eventful day across the nation and on college campuses, as it was also the inauguration of the 45th president of the United States. There were protests happening all over many campuses, including mine, although I worked remotely to support staff managing demonstrations. I was in Tampa, Florida, participating at NASPA–Student Affairs Administrators in Higher Education's AVP

Institute. I remember waking up the next morning after being on calls all day and reading the news of shots fired at the University of Washington during the Milo Yiannopoulos visit. My stomach dropped, and I immediately went to find the AVP [associate vice president] from the University of Washington, who was also a participant at the institute. She was managing and, of course, had been working all night on the situation. After this scare, I began to pay even closer attention to what happened on campuses visited by Milo in preparation for the visit to my campus.

I was the dean of students when Milo Yiannopoulos visited the University of Colorado, Boulder. Leading up to the visit, I met with several student groups and took part in meetings with students who were not pleased about Milo coming to campus. We also organized a meeting with these students and several senior administrators, including the chancellor and legal counsel, to have a robust discussion about our options. In the meeting with the students, some students felt unsafe because a student group invited a guest speaker known for vile jokes and mocking students' protected identities. The students felt their emotional well-being was at risk because the university did not cancel the event. On the other hand, other students were genuinely interested in hearing what the speaker had to say. This became the perfect storm of clashing values, emotional safety, and campus leadership (including myself) having to determine the most appropriate course of action.

To support the varied student perspectives while also honoring Yiannopoulos's right to speak on campus, two additional campus activities occurred alongside the controversial event. One activity, Buffs United, featured student performances in celebration and affirmation of inclusion. The second activity, funded and led by student boards, featured Laverne Cox, the first transwoman with a lead role on a mainstream television series. Having several concurrent events on campus, students had choices to attend an event that best supported their values while adhering to greater free speech expectations. (Akirah J. Bradley, associate vice chancellor, former dean of students, University of Colorado, Boulder)

The Educational Advisory Board's (2017) study acknowledged that college student activism is here to stay. The Educational Advisory Board (2017) reported 1 in 10 students of the 2015 incoming class expect to protest during the college journey. Lately, student activism has been the strongest over national issues that may be out of the institution's immediate control. In those instances, the role of the dean of students is to create space for students to express their thoughts, keep the environment peaceful, and offer opportunities to engage with future change agents. According to the Educational Advisory Board (2017), with the upswing in activism over the past few years, some senior campus leaders are continuously shocked and not prepared when there is a protest or demonstration. Some campuses that traditionally have not seen waves of student activism are lately experiencing it more often, along with potentially increased student participation. In response to potential protests, the dean of students should ensure that campus values align with the protocols on how to engage with student activism. The dean of students will need to have guidelines in place to allow students' voices to be heard, protect the freedoms of free speech, and uphold safety and civility for the campus community. The dean of students should work closely with other student affairs staff, local or university police, legal counsel, and the public relations office, among other critical partners.

The Role of BITs

BITs are multidisciplinary teams "designed to serve as the structure campuses can use to detect and intervene prior to the emergence of the violent or self-injurious action" (Sokolow et al., 2011, p. 7). Naming of the team is unique to the campus community and the team's function. Other common BIT names include campus assessment response and education (CARE) teams, students of concern teams, and threat assessment teams (Van Brunt, Reese, & Lewis, 2015). Depending on the size and makeup of the institution, multiple teams can exist on one campus, such as specific teams to address low- and high-level concerns or distinct teams to address students and campus employees. Some version of BITs exists throughout all facets of higher education institutions (e.g., private, public, religious affiliated, and community colleges) and they are present on the majority of college and university campuses (Sokolow et al., 2011). A well-established and trained BIT can offer innovative action plans to support countless students through their educational journey. The Educational Advisory Board (2013) benchmark study from the early 2000s noted that very few institutions had a coordinated response team prior to the tragedies at Virginia Teach in 2007 and Northern Illinois University in 2008. Consequently, Virginia and Illinois both passed state laws making it mandatory for all Virginia and Illinois state colleges and universities to create threat assessment teams. The release of the Virginia Tech Review Panel (2007) report highly encouraged colleges and universities to implement comprehensive approach teams for prevention and mitigation of potential threats (Sokolow et al., 2011). Having a BIT allows deans of students to work with a group of experts to develop comprehensive outcomes while balancing the rights of the students and the safety of the campus community.

A BIT ultimately provides care to individuals in distress, develops creative interventions, identifies resources for support, and coordinates intentional follow-up. Careful and thoughtful attention and expertise from a variety of campus stakeholders is needed to balance individual student support and protect the larger campus community from potentially harmful behaviors. This team should meet routinely to discuss a wide range of concerning behaviors, such as classroom disruptions, signs of depression, anxiety or suicidal ideation, and threats of violence. In a 2009 addendum to the Virginia Tech Review Panel report, a key summary found gaps of communication between and among university departments: Warning signs had showed up with campus professionals and departments; however, no one entity had all the information. "No one knew all the information and no one connected all the dots" (Virginia Tech Review Panel, 2009, p. 2). More communication and collaboration became the answer to creating an intentional web of support to recognize early signs of distressed individuals and create a plan of action focused on support and safety.

Deans of students chair most BITs, and if this is not the case, the team chair will likely have one of the following titles: assistant or associate vice president or assistant or associate dean of students (Educational Advisory Board, 2013). The chair of the BIT must have authority to take proper action if needed, and that action often falls under the scope of the dean of students. The membership of the team commonly includes a director of student conduct, a director of residential life, a director of academic advising, a director of counseling, and the chief of police (Van Brunt et al., 2015).

> Leading our campus's behavioral intervention team can be a complicated role. Our team consists of a variety of staff members, each with a different perspective of the situation at hand. My responsibility is to help our team stay focused on a collaborative, centralized discussion that provides a holistic response. The group comes together very well—most of the time. But sometimes we run into conflict related to our individual lens. For instance, I cochair the team with our Campus Safety and Security director. His priority, understandably, is campus safety, and my priorities are early intervention and supporting students. However, we all recognize the bigger picture of what our BIT accomplishes, and we ultimately come together to accomplish what we need to. (Denise Balfour Simpson, dean of students, Johnson & Wales University, Charlotte)

The BIT adheres to the Family Educational Rights and Privacy Act (FERPA) but is not a team bound by the Health Insurance Portability and Accountability Act (HIPPA). This distinction is important, as members of the BIT can and should share information with those who have a legitimate need to know. Counselors and medical providers on the team typically operate through HIPPA standards, which entails a higher level of confidentiality. They will not break their ethics code to share information unless there are reporting requirements and/or potentials of serious harm. Moreover, the dean of students or chair has a duty to get others involved in the actions of the team who can assist in resolving the situation.

Concerns brought to the attention of the team have become more and more complex. For instance, the dean of students, along with other BIT members, often faces difficult decisions regarding when to exercise involuntary withdrawal of a student. If there is evidence of potential harm to self or others by a student, the BIT and ultimately the dean of students in many cases must make a thoughtful and informed decision. The U.S. Department of Justice changed the policy definition of *direct threat* in 2010 and the revisions took effect 2011 (Lewis, Schuster, & Sokolow, 2012). This change required universities to evaluate protocols and decisions made in situations where a person was a threat to themselves or others. The updated definition reads, "Direct threat means a significant risk to the health or safety of others that cannot be eliminated by a modification of policies, practices or procedures, or by the provision of auxiliary aids or services as provided in §35.139" (Americans With Disabilities Act, 2010). Removing self-harm or threat to self means it is unlawful to separate a student because of suicidal behaviors (Lewis et al., 2012). This begs the question of what the best environment is for a suicidal student. What is a university to do with a student who may act to end their own life and can potentially harm others in the process? Unfortunately, conflicting guidance and court outcomes exist, leaving administrators to make the best decision they can in the face of gray circumstances.

For instance, an honors student at Western Michigan University was involuntarily withdrawn from the university after exhibiting suicidal behaviors in 2013. The student felt the withdrawal was a violation of his rights and wanted to still attend the university and found a civil rights attorney to assist with his appeal. After several months of investigation from the U.S. Department of Education's Office of Civil Rights (OCR), the student won the appeal, and Western Michigan University was advised by the OCR to change its involuntary withdrawal policies. The decision clearly informed higher education institutions that involuntarily removing a suicidal student is against the new ADA, Section 505, Title II guidelines. Sadly, just weeks after the student was notified of the appeal outcome, the student died by suicide (Grasgreen, 2014).

The number of students entering college with mental health needs is on the rise (Henriques, 2014), and when these needs go unaddressed, they often rise to BIT intervention. For instance, the number of students with high-functioning autism spectrum disorders (ASDs) entering high school and graduating has steadily increased over the past 25 years (Pinder-Amaker,

2014). When not offered appropriate support structures, college students with ASD report social anxiety, depression, and aggression and are prone to academic and personal difficulty. However, perception of institutional response to intervention in behaviors related to mental health is mixed. A 2010 case at Spring Arbor University set a precedent ensuring university administrators should not intermingle disciplinary action with support mechanisms related to mental health (Grace & Smith, 2014). Yet a synergy exists among BITs, campus counseling centers, and local hospitals to assess students and make intentional referrals and intercede in student behaviors when necessary. While mental health professionals generally cannot share information with the BIT, the BIT can share as much information as needed with those who can then assist in supporting the individual of concern. The dean of students should ensure that BIT policies are revised and updated based on any new policy guidance. Moreover, a partnership with legal counsel is also imperative to ensure actions taken are in accordance with federal, state, and local laws.

The Convergence of Student Conduct and Title IX

Addressing student behaviors, including incidents related to sexual violence and Title IX, on college campuses does not come with a one-size-fits-all approach. As such, one cannot address the considerations of student conduct administration for deans of students without addressing the intersections between student conduct and Title IX. Specific to Title IX, the dean of students' position comes with varying degrees of responsibility. Deans of students on some campuses may work with directors of student conduct, Title IX compliance officers and investigators, and other campus partners directly involved in Title IX work to design policies and facilitate processes, while deans of students on other campuses may serve in those roles themselves. Some deans of students are involved with Title IX investigations and responses specific to sexual violence, while others may collaborate with campus partners surrounding the full scope of Title IX on their campus. Similarly, deans of students may find themselves in positions directly responsible for the administration of student conduct work, while others may provide advisement or supervision to others more directly responsible for student conduct administration. However, regardless of the complexity of the role, deans of students are uniquely poised to influence policies and procedures, advocate for students, and educate the campus community on its role in keeping the community safe.

Facilitating a learning-centered, fundamentally fair student conduct process where all involved parties are heard is crucial (Association for Student

Conduct Administrators, 2014). Providing a fundamentally fair process involves ensuring equity to both parties involved in the alleged incident and subsequent student conduct process, and campuses have an obligation to address behaviors adverse to the mission of the institution and ensure students can pursue their education free from harm. While fundamental fairness is a key component of student conduct processes today, student rights, fairness, and due process were not regulated closely within student conduct processes prior to the 1960s (Lake, 2009).

Concurrently, awareness of sexual violence on college campuses is also rooted in the rise of student activism, specifically within the second-wave feminist movement of the 1970s. However, when sexual violence presented itself through student conduct processes, there were little to no response protocols at the time, and fairness was afforded to the respondent—who was generally male, which reiterated the notion of the power, privilege, and prerogative inherently afforded to men within the college environment. The survivors, mostly identified as women, had limited language to describe sexually violent behaviors. In addition, women were not likely to report sexual violence to authority figures (e.g., parents, faculty or staff, police, and clergy), often knew their perpetrator, and did not define their experiences as crimes (Koss & Oros, 1982; Russell, 1982).

Fast-forward to today: Fundamental fairness involves informing an accused student of the alleged policy violation and providing the respondent the opportunity to review information and documents surrounding the allegation and the ability to share their side of the story (Association for Student Conduct Administrators, 2014). Policies and procedures must comply with applicable state and federal laws, but institutions have the autonomy to resolve complaints based on the resources and support available on campus. Specifically for, although not exclusive to, incidents involving Title IX, interim actions are imposed to ensure campus safety. Fundamental fairness, as aforementioned, means fairness to both parties involved. Standing in the balance of maintaining fundamental fairness can be a challenge, as administrators who stand in this role are often met with competing interests (e.g., victim advocates, watchdog groups, attorneys of accused students, parents and guardians, the Office of Civil Rights) and public scrutiny (Association for Student Conduct Administrators, 2014; Brown, 2018).

For instance, the University of Virginia recently made significant changes to how it manages sexual assault complaints, as the Office of Civil Rights (OCR) rendered a decision that the institution failed to respond to complaints equitably and promptly. The OCR's investigation and subsequent finding gained national attention following an explosive *Rolling Stones* article centered on an on-campus gang rape, an article later retracted because evidence cited in the article was discredited on multiple accounts (McNiff, Effron, & Schneider, n.d.). Although not the only administrator involved in this incident, the dean of students' office was named as one of many campus entities involved in the lack of response. Although the university was able to document its compliance with Title IX, including outreach, prevention, and behavioral intervention efforts, the OCR ruled these measures were not enough to ensure equal access to education and enforcement of civil rights (U.S. Department of Education, 2015). In addition, although the university took drastic measures to comply with the OCR's ruling and to change the campus culture surrounding sexual assault, the damage to the university's reputation regarding Title IX was already done.

Conduct systems that provide fundamental fairness where students feel heard and respected create opportunities for student learning. However, simply facilitating a fair student conduct process is no longer enough to serve the educational and developmental needs of our students. We must examine, both introspectively and externally, how our student conduct processes can either enhance or impede inclusive campus communities. Deans of students' staff can play a role in shaping student conduct processes through a social justice lens. When implementing student conduct work through a social justice lens, one must consider the power structures and systems of oppression inherent within student conduct systems (Holmes, Edwards, & DeBowes, 2009). It is important to recognize how campus adjudicative processes can be oppressive simply by their design, as many codes do not recognize the various identities, experiences of oppression, or societal group dynamics of our students.

Furthermore, codes do not always recognize the lasting impact of incidents involving sexual violence and the scope of resources needed to support affected individuals and communities. As we consider the systemic structures within student conduct processes, we must also introspectively examine how identities influence engagement within the process by staff, students, and faculty alike. Both salient and indiscernible identities inevitably lead to the development of biases and prejudices, and these messages permeate interactions with others, whether consciously or unconsciously, and can send certain messages through facilitation of the student conduct process. In consideration of power structures within the processes, it is important to acknowledge that social group identities can lead to systems of oppression, and oppressing others can be conscious and unconscious, individualized, institutional, and societal. Sometimes we have the best intentions in remaining neutral in the work; however, if we do not recognize how our identities oppress others, our actions can be just as damaging. To overcome privilege or oppression toward others through these interactions, we must acknowledge how our biases and prejudices show up in our daily work and strive to move beyond oppression toward inclusion. We also must recognize societal systems (e.g., sexism, racism, and other –isms through education, media, criminal justice systems, etc.) also perpetuate oppression (Holmes et al., 2009). This includes identifying stereotypes regarding who are survivors or victims and perpetrators as they relate to Title IX. While we can introspectively develop our own critical consciousness, we must also work together in an active way to stop oppressive societal messages from pervading our process.

Sexual violence continues to be a widespread and pervasive issue across college campuses. One in five women are assaulted in college, and research related to sexual violence on college campuses continues to confirm prior studies (White House Task Force to Protect Students From Sexual Assault, 2014). Legislation has recently turned its focus to how institutions identify and respond to sexual violence, looking specifically at campus climate; codes of conduct; statistics regarding sexually violent acts on campus; and defined definitions, reporting structures, and support resources. Pertinent findings of more recent studies suggest a lack of standard definitions of rape or sexual assault; significant underreporting, particularly when the survivor is incapacitated; a lack of awareness education and programming; and an underutilization of due process procedures in student conduct processes.

While legislation, such as the Clery Act, the Violence Against Women Act (VAWA), the Office for Civil Rights' Dear Colleague Letters, and the Campus SaVE Act, has transformed the way sexual violence is recognized and addressed, these policies have not come without criticism (Gersen & Suk, 2016; National Task Force to End Sexual Violence and Domestic Violence Against Women, 2013; White House Task Force to Protect Students From Sexual Assault, 2014). While some believe the message to higher education surrounding response to sexual violence is clear and college campuses are now better poised to raise awareness of and respond to sexually violent behaviors, others refuse to acknowledge sexual violence is a problem or believe this matter should be left to the criminal process. Renewing attention to this topic, the Trump administration reversed the 2011 Dear Colleague Letter, which explicitly expressed the need for Title IX requirements to address sexual violence. Now, practices such as mediation that were once not available to resolve allegations of sexual violence are now encouraged (Jackson, 2017). As a result, many institutions have turned to professional associations, such as Association of Title IX Administrators (ATIXA), American College Personnel Administrators (ACPA), NASPA, and the Association for Student Conduct Administration (ASCA) for guidance (Jessup-Anger, Lopez, & Koss, 2018; Lipka, 2011) on how to best manage issues involving

Title IX moving forward. For instance, the ASCA describes five critical elements related to student conduct resolution processes, including response to reports of sexual misconduct—policy, initial interaction, investigation, adjudication, and institutional response—and recommends corresponding best practices to promote equity and inclusivity toward all involved in the resolution (Association for Student Conduct Administrators, 2014). With guidelines and expectations in flux, a dean of students must stay engaged in the national dialogue so as to provide the best service possible to students.

Balancing Fiscal Responsibility Amid Students' Unmet Needs

An institution's financial health, or lack thereof, often informs how the dean of students responds to the growing needs of today's college student. The cost of college has overtaken growth of family income for over a decade, and for three in four people, paying for a college degree is now less attainable than before (Walizer, 2015; Welbeck, Diamond, Mayer, & Richburg-Hayes, 2014). Yet college enrollment continues to rise nationwide despite the increasing costs of a college degree, and more and more students are looking to federal financial aid and other funding sources to help keep college within reach. As local and national governments consider initiatives to increase access to higher education (e.g., free tuition, student aid programs), colleges and universities are creating new initiatives to supplement students' unmet needs and provide access to basic resources. Deans of students have an integral role in creating these initiatives and are concurrently pressed to maintain fiscal responsibility, provide a quality student experience, and keep enrollment and retention rates high. Understanding the role of fiscal responsibility will help deans of students serve as good financial stewards and in the balance between student advocacy and institutional reality.

For greater context, consider that the 2008–2009 recession influenced many of today's fiscal concerns in higher education, at both public and private institutions (Barr & McClellan, 2011; Mitchell et al., 2017). Private education has experienced endowment and annual donations losses, declining tuition revenues, and lower student enrollment (Blackford, 2016; Clark, 2015; Seltzer, 2017). Federal financial aid through Pell grants and other funding is up, although the Trump administration proposed cutting Pell grants by $4 billion for fiscal year 2018, and the House has proposed a similar reduction (Mitchell et al., 2017). Meanwhile, costs related to attendance, technology, amenities, goods and services, and compensation and benefits needed to effectively recruit and retain students, faculty, and staff are on the rise.

What does this outlook mean for today's college student? As more and more students come to college with increased unmet basic needs, institutions are struggling to find solutions for unmet financial needs (Goldrick-Rab, Richardson, & Hernandez, 2018; Najmabadi, 2018; Payne-Sturgess, Tjaden, Caldeira, Vincent, & Arria, 2018), which leaves deans of students with the challenge of securing resources for students where resources are limited or simply do not exist. Basic needs insecurity, which include food insecurity, homelessness, and housing insecurity, has adverse effects on physical and mental health. Several studies from 2015 and 2016 indicated between 20% and 40% of college students have experienced some level of food insecurity, and 13% of community college students are potentially homeless (Goldrick-Rab et al., 2018). Students with basic needs insecurity have reported behavioral and attention difficulties, depression symptoms, negative social development, and disruptions in academic work. Marginalized students have reported higher levels of basic needs insecurity. Basic needs insecurity is not associated with financial independence, student classification, credit hours, years in school, living arrangement, employment, or having a meal plan after accounting for age, gender, and family income. The connection of basic needs insecurity to mental and physical health problems also suggests an underlying cause to other issues that affect academic achievement. This means lower academic performance, GPAs, persistence to graduation, and degree completion rates.

> One of the most difficult challenges I face in my role is meeting with students who have insurmountable unmet needs. You can see the fire in their eyes, their passion to obtain a college degree, but I know the financial resources needed to support the students' success and the university's limitations to assist. I try to do everything I can to get students connected to resources for housing, food, and medical needs, both at the university and out in the community. This also means occasionally digging in my pocket for a few dollars to provide some groceries for a week until we can figure something out. But that is a Band-Aid solution to a much larger problem, and sometimes I have to tell students to press pause on their college education until they can address some of their personal needs. That might be the best option for the student at that time, but that is also the part that leaves me completely heartbroken. (Dr. Denise Balfour Simpson, dean of students, Johnson & Wales University, Charlotte)

In one response to needs insecurities, hundreds of colleges across the country provide food pantries to support food insecure students through the College and University Food Bank Alliance (White, 2018). Colleges and universities, like San Jose State University (SJSU), used information gleaned from the Harvesting Opportunities for Postsecondary Education (HOPE) national study on basic needs insecurity (Goldrick-Rab et al.,

2018) and the California State University (CSU) Snapshot Study of Student Basic Needs (Crutchfield, 2016) to collaborate with campus and external partners on establishing and promoting a number of resources to address basic needs insecurity on their campus. Encompassed as SJSU Cares and under the leadership of the Division of Student Affairs, students are provided support related to emergency, food, housing, and medical assistance. Several staff members, faculty, and students recently worked together to submit funding under California Senate Bill 85 to receive $130,000 in one-time funds to assist with basic needs efforts on campus, including creation of a permanent food pantry (San Jose State University, 2018).

In addition, an increasing number of students in college are, or have been, part of the foster care system (Sarubbi, Parker, & Sponsler, 2016; White, 2018). This population of students encounters a number of academic, financial, legal, and social challenges because of the varied, or lack of, support systems in place prior to higher education. While several states have created policies to support the foster youth transition to and retention in college, this group is still underrepresented and vulnerable to challenges. Foster youth have the greatest levels of food and housing insecurity (White, 2018). One notable initiative, the Foster Youth Success Initiative, was designed by the California Community Colleges Chancellor's Office. This initiative supports nearly 8,000 foster youth enrolled in the California community college system and delivers an array of services focused on academic, career, and personal life skills. Research has also connected positive youth development programs and Tinto's (2012) work on student departure as a framework for building a sense of belonging, competence, usefulness, and self-sufficiency for foster youth college success (Demetriou & Powell, 2015; Tinto, 2012). As this aspect of the work of the dean of students continues to evolve, it draws the field closer to social work. As such, we are seeking to meet complex needs that largely exist outside of the institution. But without meeting our students' most basic needs, how can we pretend that we are setting them up for success?

Final Thoughts and Recommendations

My day can be full of surprises, from leading a team and implementing a college-wide initiative to being on the ground and deeply engaged with my staff on a student issue we need to resolve. It has been my experience that my role as dean of students is to inspire and motivate my staff in ways that allow our students to be successful. We deal with heartache and difficult situations from students who have been cutting themselves, to those living in their cars, to those who have a chronic illness that is preventing them from graduating on time. All these students matter, and all of them get my full undivided attention. The juggling act as a dean can be entertaining but also exhausting. (Nick Negrete, dean of student affairs, Otis College of Art and Design)

Deans of students have a complicated balance in both institutional and student advocacy, creating initiatives to support students' varied needs, and while doing so, they are pressed to focus on enrollment and retention rates. Herein lies the million-dollar question: How does the dean of students meet the challenges of student activism, bias, crisis, behavioral response, student accountability, and financial responsibility while meeting the seemingly endless needs of our students? Given the competing demands and responsibilities of the dean of students' role, it is often more comfortable (and less time-consuming) to do what is easy. An easy path is taking the stance that a student's lack of resources or increasingly unmet demands are simply not the university's concern. But how do you ignore students who stand in your office, working two jobs trying to make ends meet and doing everything they can to complete their college education? What about students in fear of their safety because the institution is hosting a public speaker who actively promotes offensive speech and ideals against their beliefs? How do you respond to students recently affected by an on-campus incident who did not feel heard by the student conduct process, although adjudication of the incident adhered to all policies and procedures? What does "taking the easy route" mean for these students? The easier solution may not necessarily be the right solution, and deans of students must determine the best course of action based on institutional policy, culture, resources, and expectations.

In concluding this chapter, we offer a few final thoughts for current and future deans of students navigating this complex position:

- Deans of students must be informed listeners and adept problem solvers. Effective deans of students listen to all issues and perspectives to properly collect information, effectively convey concerns, and holistically address problems. Deans of students also serve as listening ears for both students and their institutions and can convey information and perspectives as part of the university decision-making process. They need to have their ear to the ground and their head above the trees at the same time.
- Deans of students must be able to skillfully gather resources and work collaboratively with others to find creative solutions. As higher education administrators, we are expected to create opportunities and initiatives to maximize the student experience, but financial resources may be limited

and, in some cases, nonexistent altogether. Moreover, financial resources are only one aspect of creating a solution—you also must develop allies to work with you and sometimes champion for support on your behalf. When it comes to garnering resources, deans of students must be good at building relationships, creatively thinking, and pooling a variety of resources (i.e., capital, fiscal, human). While the dean of students may be charged with addressing a student issue, the solution may not be solely within the dean of students' office.

- The dean of students must think about how decisions made in one area can affect others. As discussed throughout this book, the dean of students is navigating issues that touch every aspect of the institution. Sometimes we cannot see how far the ripples may emanate from a decision we make.
- The dean of students is the connection between the student body and senior campus leadership. Constant attention to the expectations of campus leadership is vital to serve the institution's vision. At the same time, continuous attention to students is also required in being able to convey holistic information about the student experience to campus leadership. An effective dean of students must be in the weeds and be able to see above the trees.
- For the deans of students in the future, the convergence of today's millennials and tomorrow's Generation Z college students brings increased diversity, passion for social issues, tech savviness, and activism through a variety of platforms. No one can forecast where the future will lead. However, if we remain closely connected to our students, they will tell us.

References

American Civil Liberties Union. (n.d.). Speech on campus. Retrieved from https://www.aclu.org/other/speech-campus?redirect=hate-speech-campus

Americans With Disabilities Act. (2010). *Americans with Disabilities Act Title II regulations*. Washington, DC: U.S. Department of Justice. https://www.ada.gov/regs2010/titleII_2010/titleII_2010_regulations.pdf.

Associated Press. (1995). The court overturns Stanford University code barring bigoted speech. *New York Times*. Retrieved from https://www.nytimes.com/1995/03/01/us/court-overturns-stanford-university-code-barring-bigoted-speech.html

Association for Student Conduct Administrators. (2014). *Student conduct administration and Title IX: Gold standard practices for resolution of allegations of sexual misconduct on college campuses*. Washington, DC: Author.

Ayala, E. M. (2017). Texas A&M cancels 9/11 White nationalist rally amid safety concerns. *Dallas News*. Retrieved from https://www.dallasnews.com/news/education/2017/08/14/texas-am-cancels-911-white-nationalist-rally-amid-safety-concerns

Barr, M. J., & McClellan, G. S. (2011). *Budgets and financial management in higher education*. San Francisco, CA: Jossey-Bass.

Blackford, L. (2016). St. Catharine College closing because of financial challenges. *Lexington Herald-Leader*. Retrieved from http://www.kentucky.com/news/local/education/article81098527.html

Brown, S. (2018). Making sexual-assault hearings fair: How colleges train and choose those who serve on Title IX panels is changing. *The Chronicle of Higher Education*. Retrieved from https://www.chronicle.com/article/Making-Sexual-Assault-Hearings/242291

California Education Code §94367. (1992). Retrieved from http://www.search-california-law.com/research/ca/EDC/94367./Cal-Educ-Code-Section-94367/text.html

Clark, K. (2015). Some small private colleges are facing a "death spiral." *Money*. Retrieved from http://time.com/money/3731250/sweet-briar-private-college-death-spiral/

Cohen, R. (1985). Berkeley free speech movement: Paving the way for campus activism. *OAH Magazine of History*, *1*(1), 16–18.

Colorado Senate Bill (SB17-062). (2017). Retrieved from https://leg.colorado.gov/bills/sb17-062

Corry, R. J. et al. v. The Leland Stanford Junior University, et al., No. 740309 (Cal. Super. Ct. Feb. 27, 1995).

Crutchfield, R. (2016). Serving displaced and food insecure students in the CSU. Retrieved from https://www.calstate.edu/impact-of-the-csu/student-success/basic-needs-initiative/Pages/Research.aspx

Demetriou, C., & Powell, C. (2015). Positive youth development and undergraduate student retention. *Journal of College Student Retention*, *16*(3), 419–444.

Educational Advisory Board. (2013). *Responding to students of concern: Best practices for behavioral intervention teams*. Washington, DC: The Advisory Board Company.

Educational Advisory Board. (2017). Navigating the new wave of student activism. Retrieved from https://www.eab.com/-/media/EAB/Research-and-Insights/SAF/Studies/2017/34865-SAF-Activism-Study.pdf

Foundation for Individual Rights in Education. (2017). Spotlight on speech codes 2017: The state of free speech on our nation's campuses. Retrieved from https://d28htnjz2elwuj.cloudfront.net/wp-content/uploads/2016/12/12115009/SCR_2017_Full-Cover_Revised.pdf

Fuller, T. (2017, April 24). Conservative groups sue Berkeley over Ann Coulter cancellation. Retrieved from https://www.nytimes.com/2017/04/24/us/ann-coulter-university-of-california-berkeley.html (Accessed February 2, 2019).

Gersen, J., & Suk, J. (2016). The sex bureaucracy. *California law review*, *104*(2), 881–948.

Goldrick-Rab, S., Richardson, J., & Hernandez, A. (2018). Still hungry and home-less in college. Wisconsin hope lab. Retrieved from http://www.wihopelab.com/publications/Wisconsin-HOPE-Lab-Still-Hungry-and-Homeless.pdf

Grace, T., & Smith, E. J. (2014). Self-endangering students: The public policy conundrum [Blog post]. Retrieved from https://www.naspa.org/rpi/posts/selfendangering-students-the-public-policy-conundrum

Grasgreen, A. (2014, January 2). Before a suicide, OCR again tells colleges not to remove self-threatening students. *Inside Higher Ed.* Retrieved from https://www.insidehighered.com/news/2014/01/02/suicide-ocr-again-tells-colleges-not-remove-self-threatening-students

Henriques, G. (2014, February 15). The college student mental health crisis. *Psychology Today.* Retrieved from https://www.psychologytoday.com/us/blog/theory-knowledge/201402/the-college-student-mental-health-crisis

Holmes, R. C., Edwards, K., & DeBowes, M. M. (2009). Why objectivity is not enough: The critical role of social justice in campus conduct and conflict work. In J. Schrage & N. Giacomini (Eds.), *Reframing campus conflict: Student conduct practice through a social justice lens* (pp. 50–64). Sterling, VA: Stylus.

Jackson, C. (2017). *Dear Colleague Letter on sexual violence.* Washington, DC: U.S. Department of Education, Office for Civil Rights. Retrieved from https://www2.ed.gov/about/offices/list/ocr/letters/colleague-title-ix-201709.pdf

Jessup-Anger, J., Lopez, E., & Koss, M. P. (2018). History of sexual violence in higher education. *New Directions for Student Services, 101,* 9–19.

Johnson, M. (2017). "Grave concerns" over controversial Middlebury speaker. Retrieved from https://vtdigger.org/2017/02/26/grave-concerns-raised- controversial-middle-bury-speaker/

Karp, D. R. (2013). *Little book of restorative justice for colleges and universities: Repairing harm and rebuilding trust in response to student misconduct.* Intercourse, PA: Good Books.

Koss, M. P., & Oros, C. J. (1982). Sexual experiences survey: A research instru-ment investigating sexual aggression and victimization. *Journal of Consulting and Clinical Psychology, 50*(3), 455–457.

Lake, P. F. (2009). *Beyond discipline: Managing the modern higher education environ-ment.* Bradenton, FL: Hierophant Enterprises.

Lewis, W. S., Schuster, S. K., & Sokolow, B. A. (2012). Suicidal students, bits, and the direct threat standard. National center for higher education risk management. Retrieved from https://www.ncherm.org/wp-content/uploads/2017/08/2012NCHERMWHITEPAPERTHEDIRECTTHREATSTANDARDFINAL.pdf

Lipka, S. (2011, November 20). The "fearmonger." *The Chronicle of Higher Education.* Retrieved from https://www.chronicle.com

McNiff, E., Effron, L., & Schneider, J. (n.d.). How the retracted *Rolling Stone* article "A Rape on Campus" came to print. Retrieved from https://abcnews.go.com/2020/deep-dive/how-retracted-rolling-stone- article-rape-on-campus-came-print-42701166

Mitchell, M., Leachman, M., & Masterson, K. (2017). A lost decade in higher edu-cation funding: state cuts have driving up tuition and reduced quality. Center on Budget and Policy Priorities. Retrieved from https://www.cbpp.org/research/state-budget-and-tax/a-lost-decade-in-higher-education-funding

Najmabadi, S. (2018, April 10). As College costs rise, some Texas students go hungry. Will food scholarships help? *The Texas Tribune.* Retrieved from https://www.texastribune.org/2018/04/10/texas-college-tuition-costs-keeps-students-hungry/

National Task Force to End Sexual Violence and Domestic Violence Against Women. (2013). The facts about VAWA. Retrieved from http.4vawa.org/the-facts-about-vawa/

Payne-Sturges, D. C., Tjaden, A., Caldeira, K. M., Vincent, K. B., & Arria, A. M. (2018). Student hunger on campus: Food insecurity among college students and implications for academic institutions. *American Journal of Health Promotions, 32*(2), 349–354.

Pinder-Amaker, S. (2014). Identifying the unmet needs of college students on the autism spectrum. *Harvard Review of Psychiatry, 22*(2), 125–137.

Quintana, C. (2018). After spending millions on security for provocative speakers, here's how Berkeley is trying to avoid a repeat. *The Chronicle of Higher Education.* Retrieved from https://www.chronicle.com/article/After-Spending-Millions-on/243335

Russell, D. E. (1982). The prevalence and incidence of forcible rape and attempted rape of females. *Victimology, 7,* 81–93.

San Jose State University. (2018). SJSU Cares. Retrieved from http://www.sjsu.edu/studentaffairs/current_students/sjsucares/

Sarubbi, M., Parker, E., & Sponsler, B. (2016). *Strengthening policies for foster youth postsecondary attainment.* Denver, CO: Education Commission of the States. https://www.ecs.org/strengthening-policies-for-foster-youth-postsecondary-attainment/

Seltzer, R. (2017). Days of reckoning. *Inside Higher Ed.* Retrieved from https://www.insidehighered.com/news/2017/11/13/spate-recent-college-closures-has-some-seeing-long-predicted-consolidation-taking

Silverglate, H. A., French, D. A., & Lukianoff, G. (2012). W. Creeley & G. Lukianoff (Eds.), *Fires guide to free speech on campus.* Philadelphia, PA: Foundation for Individual Rights in Education.

Sokolow, B. A., Lewis, W. S., Manzo, L. W., Schuster, S. K., Byrnes, J. D., & Van Brunt, B. (2011). *The book on BIT: Forming and operating effective behavioral intervention teams on college campuses.* Berwyn, PA: NaBITA.

Stripling, J. (2017). Inside the U. of Virginia's response to a chaotic White-supremacist rally. *The Chronicle of Higher Education.* Retrieved from https://www.chronicle.com/article/Inside-the-U-of-Virginia-s/241832

Tinto, V. (2012). *Leaving college: Rethinking the causes and cures of student attrition* (2nd ed). Chicago, IL: University of Chicago Press.

United States Courts. (2018). What does free speech mean? Retrieved from http://www.uscourts.gov/about-federal-courts/educational-resources/about-educational-outreach/activity-resources/what-does

U.S. Department of Education. (2015). U.S. education department reaches agreement with the University of Virginia to address and prevent sexual violence and sexual harassment. Retrieved from https://www.ed.gov/news/press-releases/us-education-department-reaches-agreement-university-virginia-address-and-prevent-sexual-violence-and-sexual-harassment

Van Brunt, B., Reese, A., & Lewis, W. S. (2015). Who's on the team? Mission, membership, and motivation. Retrieved from https://nabita.org/wordpress/wp-content/uploads/2015/07/2015-NaBITA-Whitepaper.pdf

Virginia Tech Review Panel. (2007, April 16). *Mass shootings at Virginia Tech: Report of the Virginia Tech Review Panel presented to Timothy M. Kaine, Governor, Commonwealth of Virginia.* Richmond, VA: Author.

Virginia Tech Review Panel. (2009). *Mass shootings at Virginia Tech: Addendum to the report of the review panel.* Retrieved from https://scholar.lib.vt.edu/prevail/docs/April16ReportRev20100106.pdf

Walizer, L. (2015, June). Barriers to success: high unmet financial need continues to endanger higher education opportunities for low-income students. Retrieved from https://www.clasp.org/sites/default/files/public/resources-and-publications/publication-1/Barriers-to-Success-High-Unmet-Financial-Need-Continues-to-Endanger-Higher-Education-Opportunities.pdf

Welbeck, R., Diamond, J., Mayer, A., & Richburg-Hayes, L. (2014). Piecing together the college affordability puzzle: Student characteristics and patterns of (un)affordability. Retrieved from https://www.luminafoundation.org/files/publications/ideas_summit/Piecing_Together_the_College_Affordability_Puzzle.pdf

White, C. C. (2018). Creating a structured support system for postsecondary success. *New Directions for Community Colleges, 181,* 59–67.

White House Task Force to Protect Students From Sexual Assault. (2014). Not alone: The first report of the White House Task Force to Protect Students From Sexual Assault. Retrieved from https://www.notalone. gov/assets/report.pdf

5

DEAN ON CALL

Life Skills for the Effective Dean of Students

Anne Flaherty and Rob Wild

A s the dean of students, we are often asked how we make time to balance work, family, or personal time. Our first reaction is to laugh and exclaim, "What balance?" However, we know we must develop life skills that help us in our dean of students' role. There is no separation of work and life—work becomes life. We know we have to come home for a school performance only to return to campus for a student government meeting once the kids are in bed. We have experienced managing a campus crisis while hosting a dinner party. Our mobile phones are charged and at our sides at all times, whether we are on the treadmill, at the beach, or in the grocery store. The key to success in the dean of students' role is not to seek balance but to seek work–life integration—understanding our own stress and emotional needs, while finding better ways to delegate, lead, and empower others in our organizations.

Throughout the history of higher education, the dean of students has played a vital and central role in the lives of students. As described in chapter 1 of this book, the dean of students' role has evolved extensively over its more than 200-year history from the original role as campus patriarch. Over time, the dean role has evolved to meet the complex needs of an expanding diverse student body within a competitive higher education market, where expectations from students and families are high. Addressing the needs of all students, as well as those of internal and external constituents, "deans on call" require a set of specific life skills to effectively navigate their role and to ensure their own well-being. Specifically, some of the most challenging evolutions in higher education that have occurred in the past 10 to 15 years, including behavioral intervention teams, campus demonstrations, and Title IX, have placed the dean of students at the forefront of many crises and has escalated the need for professionals to be intentional about tending to their own well-being. Moreover, many in student affairs and higher education are not familiar with the terms *vicarious trauma* and *compassion fatigue*—conditions that can substantively affect the dean of students. It is for all these reasons and more that the deans of today and tomorrow must be intentional about their own health and wellness.

Why Is This Topic Important to the Dean of Students Today?

This section will provide a definition and context for the terms *vicarious trauma* and *burnout*, apply these conditions to the role of dean of students, and provide strategies for managing these conditions, which can adversely affect those serving in the dean role. We have incorporated the wisdom of our dean of students' colleagues throughout, providing real-life application to the concepts incorporated.

Vicarious Trauma

As first responders for student-related crises, the dean of students, like other professionals who work in the helping fields such as social workers, health-care workers, and those in broader social justice roles, may experience a phenomenon known as *vicarious trauma*. The term, sometimes referred to as *compassion fatigue*, is used to describe the phenomenon associated with caring for others (Figley, 1982) and describes the tension and preoccupation that some student affairs professionals may experience by listening to or supporting students through their traumatic events. Essentially, it is the personal cost of caring for others' emotional pain (Figley, 1982).

The evolution of the dean of students' role and the expanded scope of the work has placed the dean at the center of student crises, making those serving in this role vulnerable to experience vicarious trauma. One dean of students described this experience as follows:

> This happens almost daily. Two cases that have had a significant impact and have resulted in vicarious trauma for me involved relationship violence cases with students who were the victim of strangulation and battery. I take these cases home with me each day (mentally and emotionally). While empathy is very important in this position, it does weigh on me. It also can hinder my ability to "be" with my family, as I am focusing on these cases and not my family members, after work hours.

Student deaths, including those who die by suicide, are another common source of vicarious trauma for the dean of students. In the United States, suicide is the second-leading cause of death among people ages 15 to 34 years, and among young adults ages 18 to 25 years, 7.4% have had serious thoughts of suicide (Centers for Disease Control and Prevention, 2015). In 2016, adolescents and young adults ages 15 to 24 years had a suicide rate of 13.15 per 100,000 people (American Foundation for Suicide Prevention, 2018). When a student death occurs, the dean of students is often the frontline staff member to support the family and friends of the deceased student on campus and the campus community members. Beyond the immediate crisis needs, the dean also may be involved with the postvention support.

Another dean of students experienced vicarious trauma following the death of a student who died by suicide by jumping off a bridge. The dean searched online for a picture of the bridge where the death occurred. "I wish I had not searched for the photo of that bridge. I can't remove this image from my memory, and I will have flashbacks about this bridge and think about the student's death."

What does vicarious trauma look and feel like for deans of students? It may start with irrational beliefs about their work, such as "my job is my life," "I must be competent and perform at the highest level at all times," or "my self-worth is dependent on my being respected by everyone that I work with." Then deans may find themselves increasingly addicted to work, which limits the amount of time and space for personal time and reflection. In turn, those serving as dean may become more impatient with student problems, make judgments more quickly, and even become jaded about the work. For some deans, the negative feelings about work come from external pressures and then the perception that nothing can be done to improve the conditions for themselves, which can lead to burnout.

Although many experiences that deans of students have with students may be related to adverse or tragic situations, deans also have the opportunity to help students in positive ways. When these feelings are derived from helping others, the dean of students may experience feelings of compassion satisfaction as well (Bernstein Chernoff, 2016). Through greater awareness, education, and support, those serving in the dean role or aspiring for the dean role can achieve and sustain compassion satisfaction instead of vicarious trauma.

Burnout

Burnout is a condition that happens over time and is at the extreme end of compassion fatigue and vicarious trauma. Guthrie, Woods, Cusker, and

Gregory (2005) defined *burnout* as the "state of fatigue and frustration arising from unrealistic, excessive demands on personal resources leading to physical and mental exhaustion" (p. 111). In a study of student affairs professionals who exited the profession, Marshall, Gardner, Hughes, and Lowery (2016) found that burnout, as a result of long hours and stressful conditions, was a significant reason for attrition of student affairs professionals. In the first five years in the field, attrition is around 50% to 60% (Beech & Dickson, 2016), and burnout puts women and young professionals at greater risk (Howard-Hamilton, Palmer, Johnson, & Kicklighter, 1998).

In Marshall, Gardner, Hughes, and Lowery's (2016) study on attrition from student affairs, 59% of the participants in the study indicated they did not have enough time to spend with friends and family while in their last student affairs position, and 69% of participants did not have balance between their professional demands and their personal ones. Twelve percent of those included in the study ultimately decided to leave the profession to take care of their children at home. The authors concluded from their study that a culture of long required work hours in the student affairs profession and the expectation to put their needs of students first causes an unhealthy expectation, creating work–life conflicts that ultimately result in burnout.

A dean of students at a midsize public research university reflected on the challenges of being a mother while also serving in the dean of students' role:

> While the time demands of being an effective dean of students can have a negative impact on your family members, especially children, it's important to focus on the value-add too. Raising children around the campus environment and including them as often as possible in your work comes with wonderful opportunities unique to careers in higher education. For instance, my daughter has had incredible experiences hearing from inspirational and motivational speakers, meeting and befriending young people from all over the world, and interacting with students who model behavior and life choices that match the message she gets at home from her parents. As a result, I've seen her develop into a confident young woman who sees the world very differently than many of her peers. For her, having friends from all over the world is common, girls studying and pursuing careers in anything they want is no big deal, and the value of a college education is a no-brainer when she sees a student's hard work pay off in graduate school acceptance or landing their dream job. I often say that my daughter has grown up on campus. She's come a long way from the days of driving her Barbie jeep from residence hall to residence hall on opening day and could now, as an upcoming seventh grader, easily serve as an effective orientation leader! These are just a few of the career benefits that can be overlooked during the long nights and weekends away.

This dean has articulated how incorporating her family into her work, when appropriate, allows her to be effective in her role and to stay connected to her family. This intentionality is critical in maintaining work–life integration as dean.

Health Consequences and Prevention

A severe consequence of vicarious trauma and burnout can be physical and mental illness. It is imperative that a dean of students employs self-care strategies to help prevent these conditions. One way to prevent the onset of trauma is engaging in meditation, yoga, and mindfulness. Daut (2016) described the many positive effects of yoga on physical and mental health as a self-care strategy for professionals working in student affairs and higher education, because yoga addresses both the physical and emotional concerns and is an effective tool to restore health. However, yoga as a research-based technique for self-care has been only moderately popular within the higher education setting (Daut, 2016). Chapter coauthor Anne Flaherty began her yoga practice over 10 years ago when she was a doctoral student, graduate assistant, and mother of young children. She remembers initially being intimidated by yoga positions but quickly realized the benefits gained through yoga practice, including more awareness of deep breathing. Flaherty described, "During yoga practice, and concluding with the Shavasana pose, I learned how to embrace being present in the moment. I try to remember this feeling and carry this into my dean of students' practice." Flaherty further described that she had the opportunity to take yoga classes on campus: "I've worked at two universities where yoga classes were offered for free to staff and faculty over the noon hour. Practicing yoga during the middle of the day is an excellent way to stretch your muscles, recenter your breathing, and recharge your mind and body for the remainder of the day."

In addition to yoga, engaging in other types of physical activity is essential to helping counterbalance the symptoms associated with vicarious trauma and burnout. One dean described her passion for pickleball, an athletic activity that draws together aspects of tennis, badminton, and table tennis, and described how this activity helps her with work–life integration: "I play pickleball two to three times a week off-site with people not associated with my institution. I like to hit the ball really hard. It is therapeutic." Having hobbies with friends outside of the campus workplace provides alternative perspectives and an opportunity to think and talk about activities beyond work. In summary, deans of students are encouraged to identify a fitness activity and a personal hobby to provide an outlet for stress management, personal time, and reflection.

Impact of Supervision

Vicarious trauma and burnout, coupled with current fiscal constraints within higher education, can also affect one's effectiveness to be a good supervisor and colleague. Due to financial challenges, staff downsizing and unfilled positions may result in staff fulfilling multiple roles simultaneously. This, in turn, results in staff members working longer, unpredictable hours and managing multiple responsibilities. Supervisors, who may be balancing their own issues related to vicarious trauma and burnout, may adversely affect those they supervise because of this. Therefore, practicing self-care is not only about being the best possible professional but also about being the best possible supervisor. Supervisors can help their staff through effectively communicating, modeling self-care, and offering mentoring programs to teach skills about work–life integration. One dean described, "When I am stressed, I am less creative and less patient. Both of these elements negatively impact my ability to supervise effectively. When I am under a great amount of stress, I find myself needing to be intentional about tending to my relationships with my direct reports. These interactions help balance my stress with elements of my job that bring me joy and satisfaction."

Negative Impact on Family, Loved Ones

A familiar adage regarding one's lifetime spent working is that no one will ever say on their deathbed, "I wish I had worked more," while many will say, "I wish I had spent more time with family and friends." Because of the demands of the dean of students' role, the culture of long hours required working evenings and weekends, and the expectation to put the needs of students first, the role of the dean of students can have an adverse impact on deans' family and loved ones.

As we prepared for this chapter, we both reflected on our own careers and efforts to manage work stress that often creates challenges in the home environment. It is inevitable that work crises will arise at inopportune times and that work stress can lead to depression and personal frustration outside of work. Dean of students Rob Wild offered the following reflection:

> I remember a two-month stretch on our campus of significant student protest and unrest. Our students were very upset with the university, and I was regularly finding myself across the table from very angry students who were upset with the university and my colleagues. It was a trying time. I carried that stress home with me every night—affecting my parenting, the relationships I had with my family and my partner—it was awful. In hindsight,

I wish I had done a better job of not letting that stress carry over to the lives of those I care so deeply about.

Clearly, the negative energy that occasionally swirls around the dean of students' office can lead to burnout and affect family and friends. It takes great skill, commitment, and significant support from friends, family, and colleagues to manage that stress and prevent burnout.

Integration for the Effective Dean of Students

The dean of students, like other executive-level university staff, faces daily pressures related to student support, crisis management, decision-making, resource allocation, personnel issues, and strategic planning that can take a toll on the individual's stress levels and ability to perform the job. Establishing and prioritizing self-care strategies is essential to the long-term success and well-being of the dean of students. This section will define *work–life integration*, describe generational differences, and describe the intersectionality between identity and the approach to the dean of students' role, as well as the integration of all roles (self, family, and community).

As the dean of students' role has evolved, so have the work-style approaches of those filling these roles based on what generation the individual was born. In Lancaster and Stillman's (2002) book about generational differences in the workforce, they described the different approaches across the four generations in the workforce: Traditionalists were born before 1945, baby boomers were born between 1946 and 1964, Generation Xers were born between 1965 and 1980, and millennials were born between 1981 and 1999. Since most traditionalists are retired, this section will focus on the other three generations still actively working in the field. This section provides some context for understanding how burnout may occur across the generations based on how they view job security and work–life integration.

Most senior leaders in student affairs are likely baby boomers and have worked to "build a stellar career" and want to "help me balance everyone else and find meaning myself" (Lancaster & Stillman, 2002, p. 110). Because of the changing economy and the unlikely nature that one spends an entire career at one institution, Generation Xers understand the need to "build a portable career." Work–life integration has always been a priority: "Give me balance now, not when I'm sixty-five!" (p. 110). At present, Gen Xers, like baby boomers, are the most likely to be serving in the dean of students' role. Millennials, who make up the majority of the entry-level positions, have always understood the fluid nature of their positions with "job changing is necessary" and that "work isn't everything; I need flexibility so I can balance all of my activities" (p. 110). Recognizing there are some inherent differences in philosophical approaches to work–life integration across generations, strategies for educating about work–life integration and the motivation to make these a priority may look different across baby boomers, Gen Xers, and millennials.

In Hecht and Pina's (2016) book *AVP: Leading From the Unique Role of Associate/Assistant Vice President for Student Affairs*, they described the difference between work–life balance and work–life integration, with the latter concept recognizing that our lives are too complex to balance. Work–life integration is the approach that Friedman (2014) referred to as bringing together work and life across four domains of work, home, community, and the private self. One dean suggested a possible reality that finding balance is impossible for the dean of students:

> I have always viewed my work as a lifestyle and don't really buy into this idea that a balance is ever really achievable. There are predictable cycles to our work, and sometimes we have to be all in and other times we do not. My spouse is also part of the higher education community. When our children were young, we folded lots of university activities into our family life. Our children benefited from exposure to the environment and the relationships they developed with college students. I've been through over 30 annual cycles. I've learned not to jump at every new best idea or fad. Many initiatives look good for a short time and then fade away when the next best thing comes along. I am committed to our professional values, and those have really stood the test of time. I have learned I don't have to do everything. I can be selective about the things to which I commit my time and energy.

This position reflects a reality for many deans of students—that true balance is an impossible goal. Finding reward in the space between personal life and work means managing the pace and workload as much as possible while finding time outside of the workplace for the things that really matter. Realizing that the goal is not balance but instead achieving a rhythm in one's life where work and personal life can coexist at the same time will lead to better success at both.

Family, Community, and Private Self

No one can walk this journey as dean alone or without taking time for oneself. This section delves into facets of family, community engagement, and the importance of maintaining parts of your life at the same time as being dean.

Raising a Family

According to coauthor Anne Flaherty, the desire to find some balance between family and professional life led to a short-term stop out of full-time professional work when her children were very young and she went back to school to pursue a PhD. According to Flaherty,

> I knew that I wanted to pursue a PhD in higher education administration; however, pursuing this while working in a demanding position as an assistant dean, as a wife raising two children under the age of three, seemed like a recipe for enormous stress and would result in me not doing any of these three positions very well.

Flaherty acknowledges that she was fortunate to have had the ability to make this decision because her partner was able to support their family financially. During the five-year period where Flaherty pursed her PhD full-time, she held a doctoral graduate assistantship that allowed her to maintain some professional connection while also providing the flexibility to focus on her doctoral studies and young family. According to one male dean,

> Honestly, I don't see my work and my life needing to balance, but rather be integrated. There are days I leave early to go to soccer games with my son, and I'll spend some time e-mailing at night. I avoid weekend work wherever possible. It starts from the top. My president is supportive of my needing to get away to spend time with family, and the people who work for me who have families see me modeling the way. At times, I can integrate by bringing my family to appropriate university events. The students get to see that I support them, and I get to spend time with family at the same time.

One strategy deans can employ is to look for opportunities to integrate family life into the dean of students' responsibilities. For example, bringing children and partners to campus events can be a useful tactic, as appropriate. Flaherty had basketball season tickets, and her family joined her at the games. While this strategy can allow the dean to be visible and in attendance at campus events, there is also a need to carve out dedicated family time outside of campus life.

Engaging in Your Community

Finding reward and balance in life is not just about career and family. Most deans of students have interests and hobbies that extend beyond the walls of the institution. Sometimes it is easy to become fixated on the problems and concerns of a busy and demanding college or university community and lose sight of the bigger role that all deans play in their communities. Finding a way to pursue interests and hobbies that make a difference in one's community can be an effective strategy for maintaining balance in the role of the dean of students. For some, this can be involvement in a church or place of worship. Others might engage in community service or volunteer work of their choice. Dean of students and chapter coauthor Rob Wild reported that he enjoyed spending time on various education-related boards that aligned with his interests in K–12 education reform:

> I find time spent on education-related boards extremely valuable to my sense of connection to my region and my city. It helps me to put into perspective the important role that our university has in preparing leaders to address community challenges and support future generations. And, even though it is additional time to my already busy schedule, I find the time worth it to my overall sense of balance and purpose.

To minimize the impact on time, the community engagement can align with existing programs of the college or university. This could be working with students on voter registration drives or in community youth mentoring programs. There are always plenty of service opportunities within the university as well, such as helping keep score at sporting events or advising a student organization that is of interest.

There are some important questions for you to ask and reflect on before seeking out engagement in your community:

- How much can you give up in the way of personal time? Can you add another weekly commitment to your already busy schedule, or should you look for service opportunities that are monthly or quarterly?
- What are your personal interests in your community that give you the greatest sense of reward? Engagement interests can change over time. Are you open to taking a risk and trying something new?
- What are the needs and opportunities that exist for involvement in your local community? Larger cities often have websites that advertise not-for-profit board service opportunities.

Evaluating these questions in advance can lead to an effective community partnership opportunity that can assist in addressing work–life balance and your sense of personal accomplishment.

Finding Time for Yourself

A familiar expression, shared by flight attendants prior to departure, is if you are traveling with children, be sure to place your own oxygen mask first before helping your child. Why? Because if you run out of oxygen, you cannot help others. As a dean, you are a leader and role model for your staff and for students. This popular metaphor is crucial for those serving as dean who tend to prioritize the well-being of others, often before self. What does this look like? It includes getting enough sleep, eating a healthy diet that will help you thrive, getting regular exercise, and dedicating time daily for renewal through meditation, music, journaling, or taking note of what you are grateful for today. It also means finding something that will make you laugh! Flaherty is involved with a book club with some women from her neighborhood. She described, "These are good connections for me, as I have an outlet of individuals independent from my work life." Although it can often be difficult to find the time to read, she will listen to books while driving to and from campus. For deans, finding time for oneself should be viewed not as a luxury but rather a requirement for serving effectively in this role. Knowing and clarifying your values, which should include personal time, is an essential step in your leadership journey.

Communication and Technology

The fast-paced environment of the dean of students requires constant communication. The modern technology that is available to the dean of students has made communication much easier. An after-hours crisis that, at one time, required the dean of students to return to campus now can be handled from home on a conference call. Business that used to be done over the telephone or in face-to-face meetings can now be accomplished over e-mail, which allows conversations to be logged and tracked for record-keeping purposes.

However, improved communication technology has not necessarily made life easier for the dean of students. For those who value more separation between work and life, technology can also be perceived as a burden when people are able to be in contact with their work 24/7/365. One dean of students interviewed described today's communication technology as an electronic leash: "I receive phone calls, texts, and e-mails from the vice president or staff members at all hours of the day or night, even when school is not in session or when I am on vacation. Technology is definitely an additional stressor."

However, technology can also be a great benefit when it comes to work–life integration, allowing deans of students to do their job while spending time with family and friends. "I prefer to keep abreast of situations by text and e-mail after hours so I know what will greet me in the morning," reported one dean of students.

Our present technological reality has made it impossible to separate work and personal life for the dean of students. Rather than fight technology as it emerges, the dean of students needs to find better ways to adapt and view technology as a part of work–life integration rather than a barrier to balance.

Coauthor and dean of students Rob Wild recalled a recent spring softball game with his 13-year-old daughter:

> The director of residential life called me about a potential student crisis. I was helping to coach the team at the time. I was able to arrange for a quick conference call with key staff to develop a response plan in between innings, and I was back coaching third base moments later.

Being able to do this allows deans to do their job, while also spending their time outside of work in ways they find relaxing and rewarding.

It is important for deans of students to evaluate and sometimes change their strategies when it comes to using communication technology related to balance. The following sections discuss a few suggestions from our research and our interviews.

Social Media

The use of social media in student affairs and in society has become a reality that is here to stay. Student-related issues and perceptions of these issues can evolve at lightning speed over various social media platforms, requiring deans of students and their staff to closely monitor the Internet and respond as needed. However, not every dean of students needs to have an active Twitter account to be effective in the role. As stated by Hecht and Pina (2016), use "social media [if it] enhances your professional effectiveness, learn about social media technologies that fit your needs and the institutional culture" (p. 149). Just make sure to think carefully about the following considerations before jumping into the Twittersphere:

- If you have a public affairs office, does it have policies related to senior staff and social media? Remember, anything you say in social media could be viewed as the university's position on a topic.
- Develop a personal strategy for your use of social media. Is this how you want to connect with parents and families? Do you want to use it simply as a platform to celebrate and acknowledge students and student group

accomplishments? If so, are you recognizing the full diversity of your students and their activities?

- Remember that it is impossible to have a truly private social media presence. This is important to remember before you share your personal opinions about political matters or post college reunion photos of you reliving your freshman year with your friends. All social media is open for scrutiny.
- Set boundaries with students and social media. Several deans interviewed reported that they don't follow or "friend" their current students on social media. Setting that boundary helps to manage expectations for both the dean of students and the student community about appropriate channels of communication that don't require as much time to monitor and respond.
- Manage your time on social media. Figure out if there are ways it can save you time and how you can have a consistent presence that does not become an additional burden for you.

Managing E-mail

Although e-mail should now officially be considered an old technology, managing and staying on top of e-mail can feel like a never-ending burden for all professionals. A recent article (Martin & Curzan, 2018) outlined a strategy adopted by an academic dean's office that limited e-mail traffic to business hours, limited the forwarding of e-mails, and encouraged employees to communicate in person rather than over e-mail. Strategies like this are worth considering if they fit within the institutional culture. But they work only if there are shared expectations among all parties involved. To avoid becoming overwhelmed by e-mail, effective deans of students should set clear expectations with their direct reports about how they want to use e-mail for communication. E-mails that do not need a response should be marked "for information only," and there should be expectations for what is appropriate to communicate over e-mail versus in a face-to-face meeting. The dean of students should set aside specific time each day to read and respond to e-mails. Again, the effective dean of students should not think about e-mail as a burden but instead figure out how it can allow for improved work–life integration.

Taking Technology Breaks

It is okay not to be connected to a computer or mobile device 24 hours day. During vacations with family, at school performances with children, or simply when you need a break to read a book or exercise, create time for technology breaks. The use of the away message feature on e-mail can be a valuable tool for communicating limited availability over e-mail. The on-call role of the dean may not always allow for complete electronic silence. If the stress and pressure of being on call becomes too much, deans must work within their own team, and their peer group of associate vice presidents if they have one, to share the burden of on-call responsibilities. This is necessary for the emotional and psychological stability and well-being of the dean of students. Work to build in technology breaks. This is a tool for success for effective work–life integration.

Using the Pace of the Academic Year for Balance Rather Than Regulating Technology

For most deans of students, there are times of the year when there is a need for more electronic communication than is needed at other times. Recognizing the cycles of intensity in the dean of students' role and taking full advantage of the down times in the calendar are important for effective balance. There really is no good way to stem the pace and flow of communication at the start of the fall semester, for example. But for most deans of students, the period right after commencement in the spring can be quieter. Being intentional about using the down times in the academic calendar to limit electronic communication and to regroup and recharge is appropriate and necessary for effective balance.

Universal Strategies for Decreasing Stress and Managing Expectations

Developing self-care strategies and habits is essential to the long-term health and well-being of those leading in executive-level positions, such as the dean of students. This section will offer reflections about how we each manage stress differently based on our life experiences and provide some additional concrete strategies for self-care.

Knowing Your Values, Priorities, and Strengths

The foundational step on the journey to credible leadership is clarifying your values, discovering those fundamental beliefs that will guide your decisions and actions along the path (Kouzes & Posner, 2012). Every dean of students is different, with a unique set of life experiences, identities, and ways of managing stress. In the role of dean, you need to know and understand your own values, strengths, and priorities as you face challenges in the workplace. For example, different people have different needs when it comes to sleep. Some people work well in the early morning and don't do well when they have to stay up late. Others are night owls and do their best thinking after 10:00 p.m. As another example, consider stressful situations. Some deans approach these situations by carefully preplanning and creating checklists. Others do well managing a crisis in the moment. Deans who prefer preplanning and working with checklists will not thrive when trying to work in the moment. As a dean of students, you must clarify your strengths, priorities, and values as you approach your role. Some critical questions that relate to personal values that you should ask as you approach the role are as follows:

- What situations do you find most stressful in the workplace? Working with parents? Mediating student conflict? How have you managed those situations effectively in the past? What training and coaching can you receive to get better at managing these situations?
- What do you find rewarding about the role of dean of students? Solving problems? Supervising staff? Advising students? How do you make sure that you are finding time for the rewarding aspects of the job?
- What are your professional priorities? A key to successful leadership in the dean of students' role—a role where the priorities are constantly driven by the moment, the needs of students and leadership, and the crisis of the day—is to set priorities and maintain overall focus. Priorities shift and should focus on the big picture. Are you trying to hire and develop a new team? Is renewed attention on diversity and inclusion a value for the units you manage? Are financial and budget matters at the forefront of your work?

Understanding personal values, priorities, and strengths is critical to the success of the dean of students.

The Role of Individual Identity in Self-Care

When it comes to self-care in the dean of students' role, there is no one-size-fits-all approach. Personal identity can have a significant influence on how someone approaches balance. In interviewing deans of students about the role of identity, a dean who identifies as a woman shared, "My gender has definitely been a factor. As is typical of most professional women, I overcommit to serving on committees, doing extra work, and mentoring junior staff. These things do not help with my work–life balance."

A 1998 study detailed that women working in student affairs who were married had significantly higher levels of exhaustion in the workplace than men working in student affairs who were married (Howard-Hamilton et al., 1998). The study linked this cause directly to married women with children, an indication of the burden our society places on women to be the primary caregiver when it comes to parenting. This same study also showed that men in student affairs exercised more hours per week than women but that women were able to sleep more hours per night. This study reinforces a key notion that work–life balance is affected by one's gender identity and that, again, strategies to mitigate the harmful effects of stress should be tailored to the individual. Other studies (Berwick, 1992; Blackhurst, Brandt, & Kalinowski, 1998; Brewer & Clippard, 2002; Volkwein & Zhou, 2003) also found that women tend to have higher levels of emotional exhaustion and stress. Subsequently, women tend to leave the profession because of the challenges associated with juggling the responsibilities of raising a family while working 50 hours per week or more. When women leave the profession, we miss out on the talent and expertise they bring as potential deans of students. Conversely, a male dean described,

> Certainly, I think that my ability to integrate my work and my outside-work life is based on the privileges I have as a White male. However, I do think that there is an attitude by some that I don't need to be with my family as much because I am the provider rather than the caregiver. This, of course, is preposterous, as my partner and I serve in both roles at varying times. As a dean of students, I have had the opportunity to take paternity leave for all three of my children (all born while I was or am a dean). I realize that not every university culture allows this, but I see it as important not only for my family but also for the future fathers that will see my example and take time for themselves when they have children.

Gender identity plays a role in all aspects of our lives and is equally relevant in the workplace. We must acknowledge the role gender identity plays, while also striving to create a workplace environment that is supportive and inclusive of all gender identities.

Racial identity also plays a role in the stress of the work environment and strategies used to reduce stress and find balance. For underrepresented minorities working in predominantly White institutions, this stress is particularly relevant. The following statement is from a woman of color assistant vice president at a private predominantly White research university:

Sadly enough, my stress level as a person of color in a PWI [predominantly White university] manifests most often in my role supporting students of color and students from other marginalized identities through their own difficulties navigating identity issues. When students experience micro-aggressions or there is a major incident on campus or in the community, often I have to set aside my own pain to care for the students. Often, I have to facilitate the healing process for students while putting my own on hold. In order to manage this stress, it's important as a person of color to find other people of color in the workplace with whom to build community. It becomes critical to not only find a safe space to process but also spend informal time together in the same ways our students find comfort in their own affinity groups.

In his 2003 book *Leaders of Color in Higher Education: Unrecognized Triumphs in Harsh Institutions*, Leonard Valverde pointed out that people of color in leadership roles often have their suggestions and ideas ignored or devalued in favor of the status quo. This can have a cumulative negative effect on the psychological well-being of people of color in leadership and is an additional cause for stress and a barrier to success. To cope with and overcome this stress, Valverde emphasized the great importance of not losing sight of one's identity, seeking support through family, and identifying strong mentors and colleagues.

Sexual orientation is another identity that can affect work–life integration. According to one former dean, who is both Hispanic and gay,

As one who strives to live authentically both professionally and person-ally, my identities as a gay Hispanic man serving as an assistant dean of students were often a source of struggle no matter how long ago I came to terms with my "brownness" or came out and owned my "gayness." Though never ashamed of my identities, attending functions where we were encouraged to bring spouses or partners frequently felt like I was "making a statement" rather than simply living my life. Certainly working at a Division I research, predominantly White university and with frater-nity and sorority life reporting to me, I was frequently the only person of color, and when invited to a fraternity event, I always found pause with bringing my partner to an event. I found it a challenge to integrate my home life with my work life, again not out of shame but out of feeling the awkwardness when doing introductions. Plus, I felt I was frequently being asked to educate, enlighten, or be a spokesperson for all that share my identities. Bringing my husband became about my identity as a gay man rather than just bringing my spouse to an event like many heterosexual couples do without thought.

In summary, effective deans of students must strive to understand their personal values and identity and identify successful strategies that make them most successful in balancing the intense and unique demands placed on the dean of students.

Universal Success Strategies

Successful deans of students establish their own personal strategies for balancing work and personal life. However, there are some key universal strategies that all deans of students should consider to effectively achieve that balance.

Developing a Strong Team

Supervision of key staff in student affairs is without question a primary responsibility of the dean of students. Nothing can be more time-consuming or emotionally draining than supervising a difficult or underperforming director or senior student affairs leader. In addition, deans of students will often find themselves serving as the acting director when key leaders in their areas are missing. Sometimes this can occur during a time of transition or restructuring. Occasionally, the dean of students will have to manage a unit because of hiring freezes during times of budget constraint. Deans of students who have found themselves in a difficult supervisory situation know the stress and anxiety this can bring about for weeks or months, not to mention the significant additional time involved spent coaching and managing additional employees. Consequently, one of the best ways to decrease the overall stress of supervision is to hire and develop a strong team. Teams that are well trained, capable, and competent require less management related to day-to-day tasks so the dean of students can focus more on strategic vision, crisis management, and other higher level institutional priorities. In an effort to better manage dean–life balance, deans of students should review their teams, asking the following questions:

- Can your employees benefit from additional training or coaching that you can't provide but that would make them more effective leaders?
- Do you have underperforming employees who should no longer be a part of your team? Giving difficult feedback is not easy, but underperforming employees can harm the student experience and take a significant amount of supervisory time.
- Hiring new talent is one of the most important roles of a dean of students. Are you taking the time needed during your searches to recruit, evaluate, and identify talented and diverse employees?

- What are you doing to develop talent from within your organization, providing mentorship and opportunities for advancement for your highest performing employees?

Having a strong team in place requires constant monitoring and work, but it helps enormously with the challenge of work–life integration for the dean of students.

Learn to Delegate Effectively

Very often, one of the biggest challenges facing the dean of students is the pervasive mentality of "if I want something done right, I need to do it myself." Most deans of students have served effectively in director roles at an earlier part of their career. They know how to solve problems and are not afraid of hard work or rolling up their sleeves and getting down in the trenches during difficult situations. As admirable as these qualities are, they are not effective management strategies when it comes to work–life integration. Deans of students need to trust their teams to do their jobs. Delegating helps your direct reports become more confident and trusting of you as their leader, and it offers them the opportunity to develop the skills they need as they advance in their careers.

Setting Boundaries

It is okay to say no sometimes. Most deans of students have been successful throughout their careers by being able to juggle multiple priorities at the same time and offering to participate in the task force, lead a committee, or take on the advising of important student organizations. All these roles and experiences are valuable, but there simply is not enough time in the day for a dean of students to do everything he or she is asked to do. Effective deans are still able to juggle multiple priorities; however, they are also able to set appropriate boundaries in their work.

Family as Part of the Institution

As mentioned earlier in this chapter, it is important to acknowledge again that effective work–life integration does not include a complete separation of one's personal life from one's professional life. Dean of students Anne Flaherty talked about bringing her family to sporting events. For a dean who often has work pressures that extend well beyond a typical 9-to-5 day, the ability to integrate one's family into the life of the university can help with balance. This can include things such as using the university's child-care facilities and bringing family to student theater, sporting events, or concerts whenever possible. Completely decoupling one's family from the life of the university can lead to tension and stress when trying to manage work and personal life.

Developing Strong Professional Networks

Being a dean of students can be a very lonely role. It can be one of the most challenging middle-management positions in higher education. Deans must balance the priorities of students, their families, their vice president, their president, and their own employees. Finding a safe and comfortable place to seek support and advice related to the challenging situations faced in the role from others who understand the dean of students' role is a key to success. Often, this support network needs to be outside the home institution. There are professional communities and engagement opportunities available through NASPA–Student Affairs Administrators in Higher Education (e.g., AVP Steering Committee, AVP Institute) and several other organizations. Finding this support network can not only help deans of students realize their challenges are not unique but also provide helpful input into the complex challenges faced in today's institutions of higher education.

Finding Happiness in Your Work: It's All About the Students!

The problems students face in college in the twenty-first century are complex and daunting. Today's students struggle with issues related to drug and alcohol use, diversity and inclusion, sexual assault, and mental health issues, to name just a few. The dean of students is at the epicenter of these challenges, and the work can understandably be draining, time-consuming, and exhausting. However, the dean of students is also often behind the many success stories for students. Deans of students develop and support programs aimed at student success. They often find themselves as the advocate for students who have nobody else in their corner. Deans help manage and resolve conflict and hold students and organizations accountable to institutional values. In this hard work, it is important for effective deans of students to regularly center themselves around why they do the work—it is, after all, all about the students! The reward in the work comes during commencement season, when many happy students and their families celebrate an important life milestone. It comes from mentoring individual students and watching them change and grow during an important phase of young adulthood. It comes from following graduates and alumni on social media and through alumni programs and watching them find success in their lives after graduation. This sense of reward and acknowledgment that deans of students are central to the overall success of students—that they are a part of something that is bigger than themselves or their role—is important to remember during times of chaos and perceived instability in the role. Finding true balance means not only finding ways to prioritize and manage but also recognizing and celebrating the rewards and happiness that this role can bring.

Conclusion

As the role of dean of students has evolved to meet the complex needs of an expanding diverse student body, the stress placed on those serving in these roles has escalated. The net result of these increased demands has led some deans of students to experience vicarious trauma, burnout, and attrition from the profession. Being a dean of students can be one of the most fun and rewarding positions in higher education. By effectively managing work–life integration, the dean of students can maximize the benefits of the role while managing the elements that lead to stress and burnout.

In an effort to support the overall well-being of the "dean on call," we offer the following recommendations:

- Know the signs of vicarious trauma and burnout and help educate your staff and your vice president about these entities.
- Develop strategies for preventing vicarious trauma and burnout through dedicated time for one's personal life, including family and friends, community, and self. This includes one's physical and mental health and personal hobbies.
- Know your values and priorities and establish healthy boundaries. View your values as your personal bottom line.
- Understand the tenets of work–life integration and how you can use strategies such as technology, delegation, and the development of a great team to improve balance.
- Be present in each moment whether that is with your staff, supervisor, students, family, friends, or self.
- Recognize that there is a rhythm to our lives, with busier periods. However, developing good habits and well-being is a choice one can make to manage the busier periods.
- Remember that time is your most precious resource. Does your calendar reflect your values?
- A healthy career requires self-kindness.

References

American Foundation for Suicide Prevention. (2018, June 1). Suicide statistics. Retrieved from https://afsp.org/about-suicide/suicide-statistics/

Beech, R. A., & Dickson, T. (2016, March). *Caring too much: Compassion fatigue in student affairs.* Paper presented at ACPA, Montreal, Canada.

Bernstein Chernoff, C. R. (2016). The crisis of caring: Compassion satisfaction and compassion fatigue among student conduct and behavior intervention professionals. *Doctoral dissertation,* University of South Florida. Retrieved from http://scholarcommons.usf.edu/etd/6066

Berwick, K. (1992). Stress among student affairs administrators: The relationship of personal characteristics and organizational variables to work-related stress. *Journal of College Student Development, 33,* 11–19.

Blackhurst, A., Brandt, J., & Kalinowski, J. (1998). Effects of personal and work-related attributes on the organizational commitment and life satisfactions of women student affairs administrators. *NASPA Journal, 35*(2), 86–99.

Brewer, E. W., & Clippard, L. F. (2002). Burnout and job satisfaction among student support services personnel. *Human Resource Development Quarterly, 13*(2), 169–186.

Centers for Disease Control and Prevention. (2015). Suicide facts at a glance. Retrieved from https://www.cdc.gov/violenceprevention/pdf/suicide-datasheet-a.pdf

Daut, C. (2016). A case for more yoga on campus: Yoga as self-care for higher education and student affairs professionals. *The Vermont Connection, 37,* 48–60.

Figley, C. (1982). *Traumatization and comfort: Close relationships may be hazardous to your health.* Keynote presentation at Families and Close Relationships: Individuals in Social Interaction Conference, Texas Tech University, Lubbock, TX.

Friedman, S. (2014). What successful work and life integration looks like. *Harvard Business Review.* Retrieved from https://hbr.org/2014/10/what-successful-work-and-life-integration-looks-like

Guthrie, V. L., Woods, E., Cusker, C., & Gregory, M. (2005). A portrait of balance: Personal and professional balance among student affairs educators. *The College of Student Affairs Journal, 24*(2), 110–127.

Hecht, A., & Pina, J. (2016). *AVP: Leading from the unique role of associate/assistant vice president for student affairs.* Washington, DC: NASPA.

Howard-Hamilton, M. F., Palmer, C., Johnson, S., & Kicklighter, M. (1998). Burnout and related factors: Differences between women and men in student affairs. *College Student Affairs Journal, 17*(2), 80–91.

Kouzes, J., & Posner, B. (2012). *The leadership challenge: How to make extraordinary things happen in organizations.* San Francisco, CA: Jossey-Bass.

Lancaster, L., & Stillman, D. (2002). *When generations collide: Who they are. Why they clash. How to solve the generational gap at work.* New York, NY: HarperCollins.

Marshall, S. M., Gardner, M. M., Hughes, C., & Lowery, U. (2016). Attrition from student affairs: Perspectives from those who exited the profession. *Journal of Student Affairs Research and Practice, 53*(2), 146–159.

Martin, A. D., & Curzan, A. (2018, April 12). What happened when the dean's office stopped sending emails after-hours. *The Chronicle of Higher Education.* Retrieved from https://www.chronicle.com/article/What-Happened-When-the/243082

Valverde, L. (2003). *Leaders of color in higher education: Unrecognized triumphs in harsh institutions.* Walnut Creek, CA: AltaMira Press.

Volkwein, J. F., & Zhou, Y. (2003). Testing a model of administrative job satisfaction. *Research in Higher Education, 44*(2), 149–171.

6

THE 360-DEGREE VIEW OF THE DEAN OF STUDENTS

Penny Rue and Marla Morgen

The success of the dean of students depends on effective relationships with a wide range of colleagues across an institution. The responsibilities of the dean of students may cover a variety of functions, depending on organizational structure and the history and culture of an institution. One of the hallmarks of the role, however, is its centrality.

In many ways, the dean of students is the hub of a wheel. The dean must connect with resources throughout the university to support students, and most students know to start with the dean of students if they are not sure where to turn. This network of connections relies on fundamentally different types of relationships depending on the roles of colleagues who interact with the dean. Even in our two respective roles—a chief student affairs officer (CSAO) and legal counsel—we each understand the dean of students from very different vantage points.

Exploring how different colleagues rely on the dean of students can expand our understanding of the expectations of others and the role itself. We share these perspectives to help those who serve in the role structure their work, prioritize their time, and define their own philosophy and goals.

In this chapter, we collect the thoughts of numerous professionals from across institutions who interact with the dean of students, as well as the impressions of students themselves, and distill these perspectives into several themes. We explore the qualities that colleagues see as essential to being a successful dean of students, as well as the pitfalls they caution to avoid in the role. Ultimately, building from the wisdom of our colleagues, we provide practical advice for those who serve as a dean of students.

Methodology

To genuinely honor the varied perspectives of the many different people from different areas who interact with the dean of students, we collected direct input from individuals across the academy. To do this, we developed a questionnaire that includes the following questions:

- How does your area and position interact with the dean of students' role? On what types of issues and situations do you most frequently collaborate with the dean of students? How do you rely on the dean of students in your role?
- In your experience, what qualities are most important in a dean of students? Please provide examples of situations in which you have seen these qualities allow a dean of students to better serve the institution.
- From your vantage point, what are some of the potential pitfalls—both individual and structural—that would prevent a dean of students from effectively fulfilling the role? What are some potential strategies for avoiding or overcoming these pitfalls?
- If the dean of students could perform only one function at your institution, what would you want that function to be? Why is this function so critical to your institution? Why is this function best performed by the dean of students?
- If you could offer one piece of advice to the dean of students, what would it be?

The questionnaire was shared with approximately 50 professionals from nearly 30 institutions—public and private, 2 year and 4 year, undergraduate and graduate, small and large, urban and suburban, religious and secular—and 36 responses were received. These professionals included individuals from academic affairs, athletics, counseling and health, communications and media relations, campus safety and police, diversity and inclusion, residential education and housing, and many more. We solicited input from all levels of the institutional structure, from those individuals who report to the dean of students to CSAOs and presidents. In addition, we reached out directly to a number of students in order to benefit from their perspectives.

It is telling that many of the responses we received echoed themes already discussed throughout this book. Those include, for example, tensions inherent in the dean of students' role, the pivotal role that the dean of students plays in facilitating collaboration across institutional silos, and the personal and professional challenges associated with being a dean of students. Yet hearing the concepts articulated by students and professionals who work with the dean of students adds a fuller context and richness to understanding these themes. We wove the responses that we collected throughout the remainder of this chapter as direct quotations. In some cases, we slightly modified quotations for readability but not in a way that affects their meaning.

Collaboration Is Key: Dean of Students as the Ultimate Collaborator

Nearly all of the responses we received emphasized collaboration. Colleagues praised the ability to "collaborate and consensus-build" as an essential quality to be a successful dean of students. They highlighted "facilitating collaboration" as perhaps the most important function that the dean of students can perform. Colleagues and students saw different facets of collaboration, including coordination among the units overseen by the dean of students to facilitating institution-wide collaboration on a range of issues.

Many issues, from developing policy to addressing individual student concerns, require many perspectives. One Title IX coordinator identified that the dean of students was uniquely positioned to "connect the dots" across "multiple university silos in order to see the bigger picture." A housing administrator observed that deans of students are valued because they have the "tools to bring institutional resources together to solve student issues."

In all these situations, colleagues concluded that a successful dean of students must be "adept at building relationships" and able to "bring teams together for a common purpose." And to effectively collaborate, a dean of students must "make your colleagues want to seek your advice."

Interestingly, colleagues found collaboration to be an ongoing process, with building strong relationships as the foundation to be a successful collaborator. A university lawyer stated her conviction that a dean of students must "build alliances and true friends you can count on to have your back." Similarly, a communications specialist described the process as "building a council of trusted partners that you can call on immediately to weather a storm." One colleague from a campus police department noted that campus police and the dean of students must "build a trusting relationship and know that the dean is going to make the right decisions and follow through on some tough decisions." An academic colleague explained,

> A dean of students should work hard to be a true "citizen" of your institution. Be invested in the mission in a way that you commit to understanding the needs, roles, and responsibilities of other colleagues who rely on your

work in order to be successful in their own work. . . . Know your institution and colleagues and be committed to their success.

Naturally, many respondents thought that it was important for the dean of students to collaborate specifically with *their* area. Colleagues from academic affairs said to "get to know your colleagues outside of student affairs. You will need them." And they emphasized the need to "stay connected to faculty, build faculty relationships, and empower faculty." Those in counseling said to "get to know your counseling center director; they can be a vital consultant and ally," while lawyers said that the dean of students should "engage daily, or nearly so, with your legal counsel."

This collaboration is not easy. According to a Title IX coordinator, the dean of students must have the "ability to collaborate with multiple institutional stakeholders, some of whom may have competing interests." As such, colleagues spoke of qualities such as having the "ability to navigate conflict" and being able to "communicate succinctly and clearly" as foundational to be a successful collaborator.

Many respondents also stressed flexibility as an element of collaboration. One individual commented that a dean of students should be "willing to seek input from a variety of stakeholders and . . . understand that often in the student affairs realm there is no single solution to a problem and that different approaches can yield good outcomes." And a student commented that a dean of students must "always go into a conversation to work together on a solution, not defend a prior opinion or position."

A seasoned faculty member offered specific advice about how best to work through a student issue with a faculty member:

> I find it especially encouraging when the dean demonstrates the ability to explore alternative approaches to issues confronting students or faculty in their relationships with students. A helpful strategy is to simply ask, "What approach on my part do you think would be most helpful?" This would allow the faculty member to express their request up front as a starting point in the problem-solving. When there are policy restrictions, I appreciate when the dean explains the policy and welcomes thoughts about how we might approach an issue with the boundary conditions presented by the policy issue. Shared problem-solving is especially encouraging.

There is a limit to flexibility as well. Other respondents offered that a dean of students must be assertive, firm, and "flexible but without compromising values." They must be "someone that can walk into a room and connect with whomever they need to talk with, while still commanding respect."

Moreover, a dean of students must have the "ability to discern when it is time to collect information [and] perspectives and when it is time to take action." One CSAO also cautioned that the dean shouldn't "assume the role has more importance than other peer roles" or "trample on other people's roles and responsibilities."

Creating Alignment: Dean of Students as Institutional Leader

The dean of students needs to collaborate horizontally across the institution, and colleagues must recognize that they should also provide vertical leadership within their area. Close alignment between the dean and the CSAO is imperative to facilitate this. The CSAO must represent the voice of the student in institutional decision-making, usually at the cabinet level. The CSAO relies on the dean to provide a range of student perspectives to inform them in this regard. While the dean must have a voice and values, being closely aligned with the priorities of the CSAO is essential. This relationship is so important that it is worth a candid conversation between the dean and the CSAO about role alignment and differentiation. For example, whose role is it to be the face of a hard decision? The vice president may need to serve as a backstop so that nonessential concerns do not land on the president's desk. That reality may affect the role of the dean. One pitfall noted by a president is if the role is not carefully defined as it relates to the CSAO, and a counseling colleague sees a challenge in not being given the authority or freedom to react and respond independently. A direct report also cautioned against "giving the dean too many responsibilities without appropriate staffing or funding to be successful." It is up to the CSAO to guard against these pitfalls.

In many ways, the dean of students is a bridge between senior administration and staff members who are closer to the ground and working directly with students. But as one colleague noted, the dean "would not be as effective if they did not have the support of the vice president or other administrative personnel."

A successful dean of students has the "ability to work well at every level of the university." A CSAO noted that the role is broad, and "the staff you build around you is very important." A direct report of a dean of students commented,

> I rely on the dean of students for guidance on the response, advice as to how to navigate the university systems, who to include in various conversations, and identifying resources and providing other context that I am not

aware of, based on conversations she is in, at her level, that I would not be a part of.

The dean of students must be able to support, and advocate for, the staff:

> The areas that report up to the dean of students often work long hours in high-stress situations, and the dean of students needs to be able to shoulder the load, be a protective barrier between middle management and senior leadership, and keep the staff engaged in the work.

This support means being attentive to maintaining staff morale and providing "multifaceted supervision of many areas with attention to detail while still avoiding micromanagement." The dean of students must try to "incorporate best practices without the staff feeling marginalized."

A university counselor offered her observation that

> the [dean of students] does a great deal more management of people than most know, thus the positive qualities of a collaborative servant leader are great qualities for a [dean of students]. An example is when there are student crises, [the dean must] be the lead person but collaborate to develop a strategic plan in response and trust the staff to carry out the vision.

A direct report cautions that a new dean may face a special challenge. "It is unrealistic to expect the dean to create change when the individuals they have inherited have been working in their positions for decades." Ultimately, deans of students must be a leader across the institution and within their own team.

A Clearinghouse of Knowledge: Dean of Students as Information Source

The practice of student affairs has become increasingly complex, and colleagues and students alike expect the dean of students to have a deep and wide-ranging knowledge base. Colleagues identified that a successful dean of students has a "breadth of perspective."

Some concluded that the most competent deans of students are those who have developed expertise along their career path:

> Often a person who serves as the dean of students has broad experience in crisis response through previous positions in residence life/housing and student conduct and can build direct connections with students to understand and work to enhance the broad student experience. The dean of students

as a knowledgeable, adept, experienced, and competent generalist is key to success in the position.

Certainly, this knowledge base must include deep institutional knowledge. Colleagues commented that a dean of students must have a "comprehensive knowledge of the university's complex history" and "a deep and wide perspective on the institution's history, culture, and values." More specifically, colleagues and students observed that knowing the "campus culture in and out" allows a dean of students to effectively assist individual students, coordinate response to acute or crisis incidents, and help shape policy affecting students.

More generally, however, many colleagues cited their reliance on the dean of students as the subject matter expert in numerous areas relating to students. Colleagues spoke about how the dean of students must stay at the "forefront of trends" in student development. A colleague from academic administration indicated that she relies on the dean of students to "provide feedback on . . . professional development needs for faculty and staff in the academic units." Similarly, an athletics administrator commented that the dean of students "meets with our coaching staff and administrators once or twice a year to discuss trends and issues that all students face as well as provide guidance on how to handle those issues." A communications specialist shared that he relies on the dean of students "to advise university leadership on both facts (what's happening) and perspectives (what students are saying and thinking)."

Together, it is clear that colleagues from all corners of the institution regularly turn to the dean of students to be a subject matter expert on all things student related. In short, as one CSAO remarked, the dean of students must "continue to be educated on all the student issues facing us in the twenty-first century."

Colleagues also expressed that a dean of students must be knowledgeable in matters of diversity, social justice, and privilege in order to be effective. Colleagues cited "training in oppression and social justice" and an understanding of "diversity at a fundamental level" as critically important for a dean of students to be effective. This work is not easy. As one colleague noted,

> Do not burden others to educate you if you are not willing to put in the work to educate yourself. Learn about undocumented students, students of color, students with disabilities, LGBTQ communities, first-gen students, students who grew up in foster care, veterans, reentry students. Know your

privilege. Own it. Do not defend it or make excuses about it. The students you serve are observing.

Colleagues explained that this perspective was so important because, for example, a dean of students who was working with an individual student to address an issue would need to recognize that "certain at-risk populations have less social and cultural currency with which to negotiate institutional structures and engage in self-advocacy." A colleague serving in the diversity and inclusion space praised her dean:

> One of the things I admire most about our dean of students is his ability to differentiate between equality and equity. There have been times in previous institutions when the need to "treat everyone fairly" (i.e., the same) disproportionately negatively affected the most marginalized students. The application of the classic "challenge and support" model evenly for all students does not serve marginalized students well, who already come to our campuses with so much challenge.

Clearly, both a breadth and depth of knowledge, including diversity matters, provide a solid foundation for being successful in the dean of students' role.

Walking With Students: Dean of Students as Student Advocate

Colleagues and students also emphasized that a dean of students must genuinely care for, respect, and enjoy working with students. Qualities such as compassion, a willingness to listen to and understand students, "deep empathy," and the "ability to easily relate to students" were repeatedly cited as absolutely essential qualities of a dean of students. A student affairs assistant/ associate vice president (AVP) summarized that a dean of students must have a "philosophy of care."

Repeatedly, students, especially, emphasized that it is important for deans of students to "put themselves in a student's shoes" and "think like a student" or to treat students themselves as the "experts." A president indicated that he relies on the dean of students to get "a pulse of the student community" and "advise senior leadership" on issues related to students, both of which require that the dean have strong relationships with students to inform those perspectives.

Colleagues and students also highlighted approachability as imperative for working with students successfully. One respondent recognized that "too often, students are embarrassed or are afraid of or lack trust in student affairs professionals, and the best ones are able to comfort, listen, and support students in distress," especially "the most vulnerable and needy students." Some colleagues recognized that the dean of students—as the "first stop for students in distress"—is uniquely positioned to serve in this role. Indeed, a university counselor stated that in her experience, the dean of students can "engage students at risk to become involved with the campus when counseling cannot."

Students appreciated that deans of students would "make themselves visible and heard in person." They advised that the dean of students must "always make sure that there is room in his schedule to meet with students one-on-one every so often. It is important that his schedule not become so busy that he is unable to talk with the students that he serves." In fact, students lamented that developing meaningful relationships with students is often overlooked as being absolutely pivotal to be a dean of students:

> Students are appreciative and grateful to know that the dean of students actually cares about the students on campus and wants to help them succeed. Being committed to serving a body of college students is not an easy job, but where there is effort, there is appreciation, and it makes a difference. The commitment and the willingness to understand students beyond their student identification number opens up doors of trust not only from students but from their support system as well.

Students referred to deans of students as excellent advisers, mentors, and friends. They commented that the best of deans of students had a "willingness and strong drive to make a difference in the lives of students." Students further reminded that the dean of students can be vital to students' development outside their traditional roles by "playing the role of matchmaker, connecting students to one another and opportunities to pursue interests and gain exposure to new perspectives."

One student reflected that although his interactions with the dean of students began in the context of a student conduct issue, the dean of students leveraged this experience to create a unique mentoring opportunity that "came at a pivotal time in my personal development and honestly played a tremendous role in helping me transition to a completely new path; one that offers tremendous opportunity and has transformed me into a new person." This concept of conduct as an element of student advocacy was also echoed by colleagues. One individual appreciated that a dean of students "can have difficult conversations with students, especially around accountability. Discipline is part of the learning process, and educational moments are everywhere. How a student leaves their office makes a difference."

It was clear from their passionate responses that students relished the close connections they had formed with their dean of students:

> I had a very close relationship with the dean of students. I met with her as much as possible to explore ideas, reflect on the state of the university and recent campus events, process issues that were troubling me, discuss personal values and goals, and LISTEN—I always loved hearing about her experiences and learning from her unique path. . . . Because she knew me so well, the dean of students was an excellent adviser throughout my undergrad experience; she had an amazing knack for knowing what I was thinking before I fully understood myself and then asking questions to help me reach new conclusions.

This is a deeply personal connection. One student observed that successful deans of students would

> listen and share with the goal to connect meaningfully with their students. Sharing their own journey—mistakes and lessons learned—can be humanizing and help students relate and learn from their dean of students. The more a dean of students is willing to share, the more likely the students will be to share. Rich connection stems from trust and shared experiences.

They also valued when the dean of students forged a long-term commitment to relationships with students, not just a transactional approach:

> During my time in college, the dean of students was consistently there for me—cheering me on loudly and proudly in moments of personal triumph, and inspiring me to reach higher, while being just as consistently engaged in my most trying moments, when I questioned my purpose and presence at the university. Such consistency is critical because it is deeply tied to trust, which is the basis of meaningful relationships. Students must know the dean of students is on their team through thick and thin, forever in their corner as they navigate unknown waters academically and personally.

The Advocacy Tightrope: Dean of Students as Administrative Liaison

The dean of students must be a "voice for students," representing the interests of all students. At a fundamental level, the dean of students must have a "vision for supporting the well-being of students." A vice president for marketing and communications noted, "In my experience working with this role, when the dean of students is proactively engaged in programs that improve health and safety of our students, the impact is immeasurable." However, it can be more than a little challenging to "always be the voice of the student in every room that you are in." While students and administrators alike generally agree that the dean of students "should be the best advocate a student can have," what that means in practice can be quite complex.

At its core, as noted by a colleague, the dean of students' job is to "bridge the student experience with the administrative experience and represent the voice of students without losing sight of the needs and responsibilities of the institution." Whether deans of students are helping individual students navigate campus systems and resources or using their "power and ability to change things" to advocate for students at a more global level, the ability "to see situations from multiple perspectives" is a powerful tool to effectuate meaningful student advocacy.

This dynamic plays out in myriad situations. For example, when managing a student protest, the most successful dean of students "manages to be an advocate as well as a university representative." Similarly, when dealing with safety matters, a dean of students may advocate for an individual student's needs, but, as a campus security professional reminded, it is important for the security team to know that campus security and the dean of students are "part of the same team."

Perhaps, then, as one student noted, the dean of students' job is simply to make sure that students' "voices, stories, and experiences are valued and accounted for in university decisions." Indeed, "the dean of students is ideally positioned for this function because they are in tune with the students' needs and attitudes and also have a relationship with administration."

Of course, advocating for students does not always mean blindly agreeing with them. A colleague in athletics opined that empathy is often best doled out "with a firm hand and a strong dose of reality." But it often falls to the dean of students to help students understand institutional values and perspectives and to help administrative colleagues understand students' needs and viewpoints. This balancing act often puts the dean in a lonely or an uncomfortable place, and yet it is an essential element of the role.

As one academic colleague observed,

> If they veer too much to one end—saying yes to most student requests without taking into account the big picture—or the other—being totally tied to a literal interpretation of rules—they will fail. To avoid this, they need as much knowledge as possible about the institution as a whole,

and they need to communicate with colleagues within and outside of the [dean of students] and student affairs.

In the words of a student,

> I believe the best ideas and solutions can potentially be drowned out by relying too much on policy without a reasoning behind its purpose. I think when it comes to disciplinary hearings, a leader should always be able to justify their rulings without saying, "Well, that's our policy."

Another academic colleague put it this way:

> I find it most challenging when the dean has a rigid approach to resolving an issue or has what feels like an overreliance on narrow interpretation of institutional policy or law. At the same time, I find it especially encouraging when the dean demonstrates the ability to explore alternative approaches to issues confronting students or faculty in their relationships with students.

On the other hand, a university counsel noted how a dean could go awry in a conduct case by

> becoming emotionally invested in a result or conclusion rather than commitment to a fair and care-infused process. Train investigators, assistant deans, and directors in both trauma-informed care and due process. It is a very difficult balance but necessary. Avoid using particular cases with particular parties as statements of broader trends or political movements. This can often result in treating persons as props and also create political backlash against individuals involved.

A communications colleague further represented the need for balance:

> Bridge the student experience with the administrative experience—represent the voice of students without losing sight of the needs and responsibilities of the institution. This allows the VP for campus life or equivalent [dean of students] supervisor to focus bigger picture, including on interactions with boards and councils.

One public affairs colleague summarized the issue as follows:

> Lack of knowledge about student issues and lack of trust by students would be disqualifying. A dean of students has to figure out that very difficult-to-define balance between being an advocate for students and representing the administration during challenging times.

There is also tension between advocating for students as a whole and advocating for the needs and situations of individual students. One of the essential challenges in the position is balancing the twin values of justice and care. Fundamental fairness and consistency are important to uphold, yet individual circumstances can sometimes call for a more nuanced approach. Thus, while respondents spoke of the need for a dean of students to "ensure even-handed treatment of similarly situated students," others commended those who know how to appropriately customize individual solutions for individual students, including navigating policy exceptions.

For example, as a faculty administrator explained, deans of students advocate for students generally when they participate in a cross-functional conversation about developing a fair and workable policy on medical withdrawals. Once that policy exists, however, they may advocate for individual students in working with colleagues to approve an exception to that policy. It is the responsibility of deans of students to "understand the relevant policies inside out so that they know how to bend them appropriately when necessary."

This tension between consistency and individualized approaches has multiple dimensions and can have implications for a dean of students' credibility with all students or with specific student populations. A housing administrator observed,

> The number-one quality of a dean of students, important in the role I serve, is to listen and be consistent in a response, while always taking into account each individual circumstance that has brought an issue to the attention of the dean—basic advocacy. Students talk, and if one student receives an X and another a Y, the word will quickly get out that the dean is not fair. Fairness is important to students.

However, consistency has its limits. A colleague with a background in diversity and inclusion explicitly made a plea for deans of students to recognize and leverage their multipartiality: "Don't be afraid to practice multipartiality! While neutrality seems like it would be the fairest policy, in an environment of structural inequality, neutrality will invariably perpetuate disadvantage for the most marginalized and continue unseen advantages for the privileged." Diverse student leaders agree:

> The work you do makes an impact that is felt by those who know about your efforts and work and by those who do not know about it. Continue advocating for the underrepresented students and serving as an ally for these communities; it says and means a great deal both to the students that

know you choose to be in this position and to administration who see your efforts and allyship firsthand or otherwise.

This principle of serving underrepresented students can play out in various, sometimes unexpected, ways. For example, there is a growing tension on many campuses about the place of the voices of conservative students, who may feel marginalized on campus. The dean of students must make sure that these students know the dean as a resource for both fair treatment and ways to elevate their voices through student organizations and sponsoring speakers. In the end, deans of students must carefully manage the many dimensions of their role.

Out and About: Dean of Students as a Member of the Campus Community

Many colleagues and students spoke about the larger role that the dean of students must play in the campus community. On today's campus, being visible is an important aspect of being a dean of students. For example, an athletics administrator praised the dean of students at her large public institution for regularly attending games and participating in other athletics activities such as banquets and celebrations. A colleague serving in the diversity field offered,

> Students need to know who their dean of students is. This can be a presence at not only events and programs but also meetings or workspaces where students are. Also a social media presence. Students are online and connected to technology.

Having a presence on campus allows deans of students to be more effective at fulfilling two of their core responsibilities: supporting students in crisis or distress and having the pulse of the campus community. By being part of the fabric of the campus, the dean of students becomes more available and approachable, two qualities that, as discussed earlier, are pivotal for being a successful student advocate.

As a colleague reminded, "It is important that the dean of students is seen as a resource and support system for all students, not just the person they must face when things go wrong." One student even offered that the dean of students needs "to be a transformative leader to create a collaborative community that is all there to help one another." A recent alum recalled,

> From lunches and watch parties to life chats on the couch and walks around campus, it is critical that the dean of students is an active participant in

campus life and models such engagement for the students. During my undergrad, some of my favorite moments were bumping into the dean of students at an event that excited us both or sitting down for lunch to delve into our latest experiences and all of the questions they prompted. An influential dean of students shares in the students' daily experience and enthusiastically challenges the students to dream and think through the academic and extracurricular paths they can take or create to achieve those dreams.

Participation in the life of the campus also gives deans of students an opportunity to further hone their "broad understanding of institutional context." This understanding is pivotal to a dean of students' ability to connect with others: "If a dean of students does not know how to interact due to lack of connection or understanding of a community, it's obvious to students and colleagues."

Having a strong institutional context also contributes to the dean of students' ability to encourage collaboration across various areas, for example, in bringing various resources to bear to support a student. As a colleague advised, "Relationship building, . . . which means being in different spaces, attending programs and events, and being present, . . . helps to create a positive and seamless experience for students."

Finally, on a deeper level, colleagues shared that in their experience, the most successful deans of students truly embody institutional values in their day-to-day involvement with the campus. One vice president observed that "culture is critical for success" and that it is important for the dean of students' personal values to align with institutional values.

Campus involvement thus becomes a concrete opportunity to model these institutional values, such as community engagement. A colleague suggested that it does not really matter *how* deans of students get involved with the institution, just that they find something that they are passionate about and engage with institutional activities at some level. This serves the dual purpose of increasing engagement of deans of students themselves and also modeling the benefit of engagement and "following one's passion" for students.

What Is It That You Do Again? Defining the Dean of Students' Role

The dean of students wears multiple hats. In fact, when asked what single function is most central to the dean of students, one respondent concluded that that was an "impossible question to answer." Perhaps because the dean of students' role is so varied and fluid, it can often be difficult to define. A colleague described the dean of students as a "clearinghouse." Another likened the dean of students to a family doctor:

> The dean of students tends to be a place where students and administrators go for all their ailments. The dean of students needs to understand the acute needs of each patient and either treat with a bag of skills or make an appropriate referral to a specialist.

On most campuses, however, "the dean of students is the most recognizable role at the institution, and students instinctively reach out to the dean of students when they don't know where else to turn." For a new dean, a communications colleague recognized,

> Whether it is a fair expectation or not, it is integral that a dean of students develops a rather quick working understanding of the campus culture to include nuances of various audiences, including administration, students, parents, faculty, and staff. A listening tour among audiences is a good place to begin building rapport and establishing trust where it is immediately needed.

As one direct report noted,

> Because the dean of students is a generalist, they can navigate across campus boundaries, with the schools and colleges, with various units and offices, with students, with university leadership. They don't have any clinical limitations (as someone in a health center or counseling center would in terms of confidentiality, services they can provide, clinical training, etc.); they have a broad understanding of students and the campus community; they can navigate university systems; and they can develop relationships with parents, students, leadership, staff, and other important constituents.

A student elevated the importance of the role of community development as it relates to what is most important:

> I think this one function should be to work with students and administration on projects that enhance, improve, and enrich students on campus. These projects can focus on different pockets of student life, such as working with different student organizations to advance an issue or different centers such as the LGBTQ+ Center to discuss new initiatives that might happen to improve students' experiences on campus. This function is critical to any university, as it promotes student growth and shows students that the administration cares for them, their ideas and needs, and shows they

will work toward these agreed-upon goals to improve the university experience for these students and for the university as a whole.

While there is no doubt that the dean of students' span of control varies across campuses, there seems to be significant agreement on the most essential function that the dean performs: fostering the well-being of individual students. The dean of students is the hub of a wheel for "students who are struggling or in crisis situations," offering "highly responsive early warning systems for discovering individual students in distress." As one colleague noted, "A campus is a stressful place and can have a very negative impact on students' health, both physical and emotional, and this can have a ripple effect in their ability to function in class but also can lead to safety issues on campus." One student stated it this way:

> If the dean of students could perform only one function, it would need to be meeting with students who are struggling in crisis situations. This function is extremely critical, and students' health and confidence need to be a top priority.

On many campuses, the dean of students chairs the student CARE team, where support for students is coordinated across multiple offices. A counseling colleague noted that the "management of the students of concern committee and its actions is most critical and best placed in this person's role in most institutional structures." Sometimes that role becomes one of student advocate, making sure that systems work on behalf of students and take individual needs into account.

While a focus on individual students of concern is essential, it cannot be the whole focus of the role. Deans need public, positive roles on campus to help contribute to the visibility of the post and to underscore their investment in a healthy, vibrant community for all students. One direct report to a dean summed up this balance well:

> One significant pitfall would be to not recognize the breadth and depth of the dean of students' work and "pigeonhole" the work into only crisis management. In reality, the focus of a dean of students should be on student development writ large, which means there are a number of functional areas that could report to or be part of the dean of students' portfolio (depending on the structure of the institution and division). The dean of students is the ultimate generalist on campus and has significant knowledge and skills to contribute to a variety of conversations. It is critical that the dean of students is engaged in conversations where contributions are valued and appreciated. This can be a challenge, because often others on campus want to know or understand specifically what a person's work is; being

a generalist is difficult in that others may not understand why the dean of students is engaged in certain conversations if they do not have a good understanding of the dean of students' work. The dean of students does not often have just one area of expertise but rather should be recognized and positioned to contribute to broader conversations about a variety of campus issues that affect students and to help coordinate support services for students facing a variety of critical incidents or crises. A successful dean of students' portfolio should encompass other areas that provide support to students directly and those that are responsible for addressing student behavioral issues and concerns, not just crisis response.

Given the wide variety of functions and responsibilities over which a dean of students may have oversight, it may be that others have a limited view of the dean's role, which is defined by their own role and interactions. We are reminded of the parable of the blind men describing the elephant, each touching a different part and describing vastly different textures and shapes. Some see the dean only as disciplinarian, others only as advocate, still others only as community builder. Any one of these limited views can obscure the complexity of the role and miss the importance of the balancing act inherent in the role.

One CSAO lamented that perhaps the title *dean of students* is "anachronistic," with a "residual meaning" that has lost its purpose. "I think the [dean of students] title oversimplifies what has become an exceedingly complicated and complex organization on most campuses and has little meaning to students, families, and even faculty." While most of our respondents agree that the dean is the person most responsible for overseeing the needs of students in distress, this CSAO noted that this perspective "pigeonholes the role into an old-fashioned depiction of student affairs in general." Echoing the many different perspectives we have heard throughout this chapter, this CSAO called for "updated definitions, cross-campus clarity in meaning and purpose, and messaging that highlights the importance of the role."

Ultimately, it can often be up to deans of students themselves to make sure that they are their own best advocate for defining and being "able to articulate the benefits of their area for the campus community." One professional working in the dean of students' office advised,

> Develop a succinct, clear way to help others understand your role and the scope of work that is included in your portfolio. Don't let others define your work for you, based on their experience or the interactions they have with you or have had with a dean of students previously; help them to see the broad set of work that you have experience in and can contribute to on your particular campus.

This Job Is Hard! Appreciating the Complexities of the Dean of Students' Role

Colleagues from all areas of campus—and students alike—recognized not only that the dean of students' role is extraordinarily complex in terms of diversity of functions but also that the tasks within the dean of students' sphere of responsibility are themselves often complicated or emotionally fraught. A university lawyer noted that "nearly all issues for the dean are complicated, with emotionally involved stakeholders." Colleagues commented that a dean of students must be "able to move on a moment's notice to resolve problems," "remain grounded in the midst of a crisis," be "able to finesse political issues and parents," and be a "sophisticated detective of nuance." More simply, colleagues recognized that it was a "hard job" and that the dean of students is the person who has to "get up in the middle of the night to deal with" all manners of serious situations. And as a president observed, "Don't take the job if your purpose is to wait for the vice president to retire."

It is not all that surprising then that the list of personal qualities that colleagues thought individuals must have in their personal tool kit to fulfill the dean of students' role was long and lofty. Colleagues commented that a dean of students must at once be "humane and firm," have a "good sense of humor and humility," be "unflappable," and have "strong moral decision-making" skills. In other words, a dean of students must "be brave in making decisions that matter."

More than one colleague warned that a dean of students must have "the ability to solve problems, not create them." One colleague advocated for a dean of students to "be balanced and calm . . . so as to provide strong leadership and not contribute to the chaos or uncertainty" and cautioned, "Don't own every campus problem and student meltdown, but do what you can to help fix them."

There are other potential stumbling blocks. One colleague observed that "trampling on other people's roles and responsibilities" could be the downside of an ill-defined generalist portfolio. Another noted that "withholding information that should be shared with others" can result from lack of clarity about limits of confidentiality or an inflated sense of importance.

Another challenge is shared by a Title IX colleague who noted, "Working in student crises or with difficult students day in and day out can wear on one's ability to be positive, impartial, or welcoming to students." Colleagues also spoke of the need for "executive judgment" or "impeccable judgment." But they recognized the reality that developing judgment "usually is rooted in making mistakes, listening well, and inviting criticism."

Colleagues commented that resiliency, "thick skin," and the ability to get by on little sleep are common traits among successful deans of students. A colleague offered that because the dean of students is often in the "hot seat," the dean of students must "learn how to compartmentalize professional obligations with one's personal life . . . not take things too personally and take comfort in the fact that you know you are there for the students." But in the end, it pays off. As one student concluded,

> You get out what you put in. This is a personal family motto, but I believe it rings especially true for the dean of students' role. The more you invest in your students, the more meaningful your relationships will be and the more the students will thrive at the university. There is nothing comparable to time and care—when students know you believe in them and have their best interest in mind, their potential soars.

Takeaways

We found great wisdom in the variety of perspectives shared with us by campus partners, and we will conclude with offers of advice to our colleague, the dean of students.

- Relationships are key. The dean must rely on collaborations with partners in virtually every facet of the campus. Taking the time to first understand others' viewpoints can yield the most productive partnerships.
- The modern dean cannot rely on relationships alone. Collaborations can be strengthened with systems and structures developed across functions that can flex to the range of issues that arise. Be sure to make best use of resources throughout the campus.
- Be a student of students. Stay alert to shifting culture and know student trends. Your colleagues will turn to you frequently for these perspectives. Do not always try to be the expert, but do share what you're learning.
- The campus will rely on the dean to navigate issues of diversity, social justice, and political controversy. All deans, regardless of their background or personal identity, will need to make a concerted effort to reach out to marginalized communities and underrepresented students to hear and respond to their concerns.
- The dean should enjoy student contact and seek it out. If the role primarily involves crisis and conduct, it is critical that the dean also form

positive advising relationships with student organizations and their leaders for balance and renewal.

- The dean is a manager and a leader, often with entry-level staff on the team. Onboarding and mentoring are key roles, and staff supervision and development are critical. Team development is also important, as a gulf can develop between those who focus on conduct and crisis response and those who focus on community development.

- A key challenge is balancing advocacy with institutional roles. A dean should possess courageous authenticity and the ability to speak truth to power, while also recognizing that senior leaders are balancing multiple priorities simultaneously.

- While deans must often advocate for the needs of an individual student, at times they must advocate for issues that affect all students. The power to do this rests on credibility that is carefully built and easily broken. Deans should be impeccable with their word.

- Take time to know the institution. The dean must be a translator of values and traditions and should make a study of the institution's history and ethos early and often.

- Deans should be highly visible to students and colleagues alike, supporting student programs and campus traditions. They should embody and uphold campus values.

- Deans must take time to understand and define their own role and then carefully communicate that understanding to others, avoiding each campus partner having an overly myopic view of the dean's role.

- The relationship between the dean and the CSAO is of critical importance. It benefits from regular conversations about alignment and differentiation, both practically and philosophically.

- The dean must learn and model resilience. The job is hard yet rewarding. Finding a way to balance the draining and renewing elements of the role is a must to maintain energy and perspective.

7

BY THE SEAT OF
ONE'S PANTS

Reflections of a First-Year Dean of Students

Vijay Pendakur

A Week in the Life of . . .

In the spring of 2018, I experienced my first true dean of students' "hell week." As Ithaca, New York, slowly thawed from what felt like an unending winter, and timid snatches of green began to emerge from lawns and trees, Cornell University's campus police kicked off the weekend with two crime alerts that jolted the student body out of any lingering vestiges of hibernation. The Saturday crime alert, distributed to all students per our Clery requirements, mentioned that a physical altercation had taken place, off campus, with Cornell students involved and that racial epithets had been used amidst the violence. The next crime alert came on Sunday and referenced an unknown person who had snuck into a residence hall and tried to expose himself to a female resident in the shower. As you might imagine, the weekend and the first few days of the week were busy for me. I worked with my vice president on drafting campus statements, helped my team plan various community support meetings, and fielded e-mails and phone calls from angry or scared parents. By Tuesday, I remember wondering if we could somehow declare the rest of the week a federal holiday so I could go home and crawl under my down comforter, assume the fetal position, and contemplate the choices I'd made in life that had resulted in my ending up in a career in student affairs.

This torturous week was not ready to let me go, however, and by midweek, Cornell University experienced its most viral Twitter event ever! Hold the applause; like most viral moments on social media, this incident was

125

marked with controversy, questionable facts, and a heavy dose of salaciousness. I remember eating my eggs and cereal on Thursday morning and checking my e-mail. I had received a heads-up from a staff member in our strategic communications area that there was a concerning trend occurring on Twitter involving Cornell and two of our students, who were being named in the tweets. I checked the tweets, and it seemed that a non-Cornell student had taken it upon himself to share a lengthy story on Twitter about his friend, a male Cornell student, who claimed to have been sexually assaulted by a female Cornell student and went on to share that, from his perspective, the university was doing nothing about it. The third party had taken to Twitter to shame the university and get his friend some justice. Along the way, he had also shared extensive details, images, and bits of personal information about the alleged perpetrator that the Twitterverse found to be compelling reading. By noon, the tweet had 15,000 retweets. By 3:00 p.m., it had reached 22,000. By 5:00 p.m., it cleared 30,000. Again, my day was spent strategizing with university executives on statement writing, fielding a flood of inquiries from students and parents who assumed that the dean of students could put a stop to this, and daydreaming about my down comforter.

Friday morning greeted me with a rare sight in central New York: a clear blue sky, so untainted by clouds that I chose to believe that the week was finally turning around, and I might just have a normal day at work, where my Outlook calendar actually represented how my time would be spent. A 10:00 a.m. phone call from the chief of police dispelled these silly thoughts. A former Cornell student, now living a few blocks off campus, was being tracked by the FBI and numerous other agencies from Homeland Security for suspicious weapons purchasing. A team of operatives would be raiding his place at noon, and the news was already on the story. By 2:00 p.m., the details were spinning out across the web: Ex-Cornell student found with a stockpile of guns, ammunition, body armor, and the components to make explosives. At this point, my main office phone line and e-mail account actually started smoking. I spent the weekend asking myself, and a few close friends who serve as deans of students, "Is this what it means to be a dean of students?!" They chuckled morbidly and said, "Yeah, pretty much."

Cornell University's Dean of Students Role: The Blueprint and My Pathway

I suspect that every dean of students' role is unique, while maintaining some semblance of similarity. Cornell University has had a dean of students' role since the 1920s, but the position has changed many times in the decades that followed. As higher education continued to grow and evolve, the dean of students' role changed with the times to meet various needs at Cornell. Most recently, from the mid-1990s to 2016, the role was occupied by two different faculty members, appointed from within the professorial ranks because of their history of caring deeply about the Cornell student experience. In 2015, a new vice president of student affairs (VPSA) arrived at Cornell and decided to take the role in a different direction by making two big shifts. First, the position would filled by a trained student affairs administrator rather than an appointed faculty member. Second, the role would explicitly focus on two functions: crisis management and strategic diversity leadership. The first focus area is canonical to the role of dean of students across the country, as we are most often the lead crisis manager for our campuses. The latter function is not as common, but the VPSA was starting at Cornell in the fall of 2015, a period of intense student activism that swept the nation and changed the dynamics of many campuses. The VPSA wanted to take a very prestigious leadership role at this Ivy League institution and have it focus on diversity and campus climate issues in order to elevate the importance of this work and to effectively respond to the centrality of activism and climate management in this moment of higher education history. The dean of students at Cornell would lead a portfolio of departments including Care and Crisis Services and approximately eight units focused on issues of diversity, inclusion, and student empowerment.

Prior to arriving at Cornell, I had spent nearly 15 years working and schooling in higher education, with an emphasis on multiculturalism, student success, and social justice education. My pathway into the dean of students' role was not the most well-traveled trail, but Cornell's unique focus on diversity issues within the dean's purview made the position both a good fit and an amazing stretch opportunity, as my own exposure to crisis leadership was quite limited. I was also attracted to the role because it was explicitly framed as the deputy to the vice president, and I knew I would have opportunities to lead broadly at the university as a result of this strategic positioning. While these were the factors that attracted me to the position as an applicant, the role has turned out to be the richest professional experience of my adult life. I have found myself challenged and stimulated in numerous ways that I did not expect and am grateful for this chance to expand my professional skill sets while making a meaningful contribution to a campus community.

What I Learned in My First Year as Dean of Students

In the following section of this chapter, I will share some of the most salient lessons from my first year serving as dean of students.

Visibility and Authenticity

I learned this lesson the hard way. If the first time I was interacting with a group of students was during a crisis, things were unlikely to go well. This was such a shift for me, having come from multicultural affairs work where students largely trusted that I was on their side, even if they had not personally interacted with me. Now, as the dean of students at a campus with a deep history of student activism, it became clear very quickly that students started with the assumption that I, as the "administration," was not to be trusted. However, if I could strategically connect with a group of students not during a crisis incident, listen to their perspective, participate in their activities, and share elements of my story and my worldview, I would become a real person to them. While this did not mean that I stopped being "The Dean," it did balance their distrust for the administration with a lived connection with me that often served as a bridge of understanding and trust in the moments of crisis.

The Megaphone and the Elevator

By the end of my first year, I had come to understand that one of the ways I could truly lead at Cornell was by serving as a megaphone for the student voice and an elevator during crisis. As a person of color and a child of immigrants, I have spent much of my adult life code switching to try to fit in and be effective in various spaces. While this was often draining and frustrating in my twenties, it turned into a major asset in my thirties, as I found myself being able to seamlessly navigate new spaces in higher education. As the dean of students at Cornell, I have learned that I can add immense value by connecting various stakeholders with the student voice by representing our students' perspectives, frustrations, and ambitions in ways that these parties can hear and understand. I often give presentations to the board of trustees, various deans' advisory councils, alumni groups, and parents with the intent of helping them really understand our students, even when they might disagree with what our students are doing or asking for.

I have also learned that the dean of students can be an elevator during moments of crisis. I can carry information and options up and down the institution, rapidly, because I have unique access to student communities and the university leadership. Most administrators who have ready access to the president, provost, cabinet, or deans do not have frequent access to students. Conversely, most student affairs staff members who are deeply embedded with students do not have direct access to the top of the institution. My positioning as dean of students allows me to move viewpoints, information, and strategies up and down the institution rapidly during a crisis, facilitating a significantly more nimble campus response, which has saved us significant pain and frustration during this period of intense student activism and strained campus climate.

Self-Care and Life Stage

In other chapters of my life, self-care for me was a big night out with friends, a quick weekend trip with my partner, or an entire Sunday spent in pajamas watching movies. As I turn 40, I have a wife, 2 kids younger than the age of 3, and a job that does not quit. Self-care has to look different for me in this life stage, but it is just as important as it ever was. Being a husband and a father while being a dean of students is a challenging tightrope to navigate constantly, but it is one that actually keeps me balanced. In the past year, I have come to reframe my family and my job, not as anchors on either end of the tightrope but as the ends of the balancing stick that I carry to navigate the tightrope of adult life. My career and my family are in constant productive tension, challenging me to stay keenly focused while I am at work and build systems so that I can delegate certain tasks and responsibilities, so that I can be just as focused when I am at home. My family and my desire to be a certain kind of husband and father challenge me to keep a healthy perspective about my career, reminding me every day that my work is important, but it is not the whole of my identity. Nowadays, holding the balancing stick of my career and my family in healthy tension has allowed me to build an adult life that is significantly more stable and sustainable than in previous chapters of my life.

One example of this balancing act is my new approach to the morning. I realized after starting as dean of students that between my being a caretaker for my campus and my being a husband and father at home that there was not much space for "me time." This is something that many working parents feel, and I quickly identified that if I was going to be my best dean of students self and my best family self, I needed some time for myself on a regular basis. Historically, I had been more of a night owl and a total curmudgeon in the morning. After looking at my calendar and my daily rhythm for a while, it became apparent that the only way to carve out me time would be to get up 60 to 90 minutes earlier so that I could focus on self-care activities in the early morning, while my family was asleep. So, I started getting in bed at 9:00 p.m. in order to facilitate the earlier morning. Now, while my house is in peaceful slumber in the morning, I work out, listen to podcasts, cook breakfast for my wife and me, and just do me. And, yes, 25-year-old me is laughing raucously at my 9:00 p.m. bedtime.

Finally, self-care for me during this life stage is about saying no. My first year as dean of students was the cosmic counterbalance to Shonda Rhimes's year of saying yes—I had a glorious year of saying no. This focus on saying no comes from an old business maxim, "What got you here, will not get you there." Many of my mentors had cautioned me that as I moved into upper-level leadership roles, I would need to find ways to stop doing certain things in order to survive the rigors of these types of positions. It is a difficult thing to do, however, because saying yes is what often gets us into these top-level roles! For years, I had said yes to numerous opportunities to present at national conferences, write book chapters, keynote special events, serve on extra committees, and take on special projects in order to grow my credentials. This habit of saying yes facilitated some of my upward mobility and, at the same time, was now going to be a source of burnout or poor performance. Therefore, in my first year as dean of students, I worked hard to say no. When colleagues called with opportunities to write book chapters, present at conferences and institutes, keynote events, or teach a class, I said no most of the time. Yes, it was painful letting all of these "opportunities" go. But all of these "nos" created the space and the energy for me to keep the focus on my campus and to be present at home. These are the two main tasks for me in this life stage, and a healthy relationship with the word *no* is instrumental to my success.

Live the Role, Shape the Role

One of the best pieces of wisdom I have ever received from a mentor came when I was entering my first assistant vice president (AVP) role. She said,

> Remember, when you start a new job, you will be living the role the way your predecessor lived it. There will likely be numerous aspects of the role that you do not enjoy, but do not confuse this with the potential of the position. Leadership positions often have a lot of flexibility on how you want to live the role so, as you learn the job, figure out how you're going to make small changes so that you transform it into the role you can thrive in.

This advice has proven to be golden, both in that previous AVP role and in my current role as dean of students. I have made a few key changes that have allowed me to thrive in the position and, in effect, live the role differently than my predecessor did.

I invested in two senior associate dean positions. One of these had already existed in my portfolio but was deeply underused, and the other I created anew. I shifted the organizational model so that these two leaders have all of the front-line departments reporting to them and they report to me. This dramatically reduced my number of direct reports, thereby freeing up significant time for me to stay nimble, student facing, and strategic. It also focused the tasks of "mid-management" in two leaders whom I can extensively coach and supervise on how to bring the best out of their portfolios. Next, I thought carefully about certain tasks that previously fell to the dean of students directly and that I am not well experienced in. I made a list and determined which of these must be done by me, for either functional or political reasons. I delegated the items that did not rise to this level to my senior associate deans, using a distribution logic that was not person dependent but rather tied to job descriptions and differing focus areas. Then I spent some serious energy in my first year investing in my professional growth for the tasks that I was not as experienced with but that I had kept for myself. This made my growth edges more attainable, as I had cut the list down dramatically and focused my transformative energy on a few mission critical items rather than trying to reinvent myself on too many fronts.

Finally, as I neared the end of my first year, I created an "acting dean of students" protocol, which was approved by my supervisor. This allowed me to actually delegate some of the most mission-critical tasks to one of my senior associate deans in the event that we have a campus climate incident, or a student crisis, when I am traveling away from campus. By creating this new protocol, I was able to leverage the bench capacity that I had created to more effectively manage climate and crisis in the moments where I felt most vulnerable: when I was traveling for either work or personal reasons. This final tactical shift is my attempt to respond to a gut feeling that I have carried throughout my first year, one that warned me that we did not have a good coverage model for what needs to happen if we have a major incident while I am away from campus. I had lived through enough in my first year on the job that I realized that part of the success of Cornell's dean of students' model was my physical presence on campus during a crisis. It is how we stay nimble and facilitate the elevator effect of moving information up and down the organization quickly. A vulnerability in this model is the reality that I sometimes need to be away from campus, for either work-related travel or personal vacation. So, I've attempted to address this vulnerability through an acting dean of students' protocol, and now when I am away, I am not anxious the whole time. This tactical shift is better for the campus and better for me. It also serves as valuable professional development for my senior associate deans, as they get to actively try on what it means to be the dean of students in some of these high-profile crises that can have a profound impact on a campus community.

The Heart of the Campus

In the spring of my first year as dean of students, I received a call from campus police saying that we had a missing student, whom I will call Ravi for the purposes of this story. The chief of police told me that Ravi's family had heard that he was missing, and his mom, dad, and brother were flying in from the West Coast to help look for him. The police asked if I could embed myself with the family so that they felt connected and supported and so they did not complicate the official police search process. I met the family as they pulled onto campus and got them campus maps. They were highly motivated to find their son and had actually called half a dozen family friends who live in the New York area and asked them to come in to help with their search. Over the next few hours, I met and mobilized a rapidly growing search party. Ravi's parents also used social media to contact his roommates, and three Cornell students showed up to help. While I was working with this group, I was receiving confidential updates from the police, and things were not looking good. We had some indications that Ravi might have been hanging out late at night near one of the gorges on campus.

I spent most of the next 24 hours assisting the family with their search, in which time I got to know them, their family and friends, and Ravi's roommates quite well. I also continued to learn details from the police that indicated the worst-case scenario. It was midmorning on the second day of the search, and I vividly remember meeting with the search party in the chief of police's office, which we were using as a home base. The search party was making a new plan for where they wanted to look that day, and I received a text from the police that said, "We have found a body in the bottom of a gorge, trying to make a positive ID, don't let the family leave for a search." I spent the next agonizing 30 minutes attempting to stall the group, feverishly checking my phone for another update. Finally, the chief of police showed up, walked in the room, and shared the sad news that rescue divers had found Ravi's body.

There were over a dozen of us crammed into the chief's office that morning, and the news about Ravi brought the entire group into an immediate stillness. Ravi's mom reacted first, collapsing to the ground as the sharp edge of grief cut through the strings of hope that had kept her standing for the past 24 hours. As she hit the ground and curled into a ball, her husband knelt beside her to hold her, and she started wailing. I was standing about 5 feet away, and what she said, or rather *how she said* what she said, cut through all my layers of professional armor and eviscerated my most vulnerable self. Ravi's mom was expressing her grief in her native language, which turned out to be the same language my parents speak and is the language I was raised with in the home. Kannada is a relatively minor Indian language, and I do not meet Kannada speakers often. I had spent over a day with Ravi's family and did not know what part of India they came from, but it was now painfully apparent. As Ravi's mom asked the gods what she'd done to have her son taken from her, her Kannada idioms and phrases matched exactly what my mother would say if one of her children were to pass away. It was singularly the most raw, personal, painful moment of my professional life.

In the coming days, my staff organized the campus memorial services for Ravi, which is part of the team responsibilities, in addition to managing all key aspects of a student death. At the memorial service, I was asked to share a few words. It was awkward, in one respect, because I had never met Ravi before he passed away. Everyone else speaking at the memorial was a close friend, family member, or faculty adviser. But I realized that in the days prior to Ravi's passing, I had come to know him through his friends and family and that I had come to feel a sense of loss for a young man who seemed to bring joy and healing to so many of the people in his life. I will miss Ravi, and I still think of him often.

As a dean of students, I am present for some of the most intense moments in a college student's journey. This intensity can be elation at students being accepted to a study abroad program, getting the internship of their dreams, or graduating from college. However, I also am in the middle of some of the most painful moments in the student journey, from student deaths to campus climate incidents that make some students feel unsafe or unwelcome. Managing all of the crises, continuing to develop my portfolio of departments, and responding to numerous campus climate incidents can easily overwhelm and erase the reality that the one key role that a dean of students plays is to bring a human connection into all of these intense moments. In this way, a dean of students can be the heart of a campus. We are the people whom students know in their times of loss, grief, rage, shame, guilt, fear, laughter, joy, and victory. We are often the face of the institution with the students' families, our alumni, and the media. In this way, deans of students play an essential role during this turbulent time in our country's academic landscape. Without a constant human element in the center of campus activism, campus crisis, and conduct processes, we risk losing the developmental and transformational outcome of cocurricular education, which is one of the overarching goals of student affairs work. These moments of contestation, disaster, and adjudication could be reduced to transactional moments where the institution tries to survive and move students along a process. Or, with the right dean of students in the mix, these intense moments can be some of the times that our students learn the most about themselves and the world they live in.

As I put the final touches on this chapter, I am well into my second summer as the dean of students at Cornell. Although I would still identify as being a new dean of students, I feel absolutely transformed and humbled by this work. Recently, a mentee of mine reached out to me for some coaching because she was a finalist for a dean of students' role. In previous chapters of my life, I would likely have focused my advice on thought leadership and sophisticated strategy. However, being a dean of students has been a keen reminder for me that, in addition to having powerful ideas, leadership is about connecting with people. I told my mentee to consider the ways that the dean of students' role would position her to foster deeper connectivity and understanding at the campus she was considering moving to. I also encouraged her to make a plan for self-care before even starting the job, something I would not have done before becoming a dean of students. Partway through the phone call, she became intimidated and asked if I ever regretted making the move into this role, and the question gave me pause. After a minute of reflection, I told her that, from the outside, it would be easy to consider the dean of students' role something to be "survived" on one's way to a chief student affairs position. But for me, this rung on the ladder has become a space to put down roots, invest deeply in a campus community on which I can have a profound impact, and thrive as a whole person.

Takeaways

- Connect with students early and often. As the dean of students, you can help your institution stay nimble during hard times, but relationship capital is key. It is difficult to form relationships in the middle of a crisis.
- The dean of students can help a variety of stakeholders understand the student perspective on hot-button campus issues. Think carefully about how you represent the student voice to various audiences. How can you reframe student perspectives in ways that will connect with parents, alumni, board members, and university leaders, given that each stakeholder group has its own way of thinking about the student experience?
- Many student affairs professionals experience burnout in the role of dean of students. How can you take a strategic approach to hedging against this possibility? What does self-care look like for you at this life stage? How can you build a professional team around you that allows you to distribute work, and expertise, so that you do not have to labor in isolation? How can you bring joy into your work, even when much of what we do can be difficult or painful?

8

WRINKLES, GRAY HAIR, AND ENORMOUS GRATITUDE

Four Decades as a Dean of Students

Sue Wasiolek

The doorbell rang, and I went to greet the next guest at the party. I am not sure why I felt compelled to answer the door; I was the guest speaker at an alumni event hosted in an alumni couple's home. In any event, I welcomed the guest, told her I was very pleased that she was able to attend the event, and asked where her husband was. She said, "He's in the car. John is afraid to come in. Actually, he's afraid of you!" "What?" I said. "Afraid of me! Why?" "Well, you remember when he ended up in the emergency room his senior year, after he had a lot to drink and accidentally cut his hand. You visited him at about 2:00 a.m. as he was waiting to be treated. I think he's still embarrassed by that." I was surprised that 30 years later this incident was still in the forefront of his mind. But, on the other hand, I should not have been surprised, as this happens often.

Having been at the same institution for 40 years in a dean of students' position with oversight responsibility for student conduct, I am often finding myself becoming reacquainted with alums who found themselves entangled with the disciplinary process. The opportunity to try to hold these young people accountable while also making certain that they felt supported was always a challenge, but it was one I embraced. So many times, I would say, "What were you thinking?" while trying to make certain they did not feel belittled. I would look them in the eye and just say, "Don't do it again. Get a grip" and maybe give them a hug.

However, it is not all about bad behavior and discipline, as I am reminded having recently returned from the funeral of my godson's grandfather. My godson's mother was a student leader with whom I worked closely in the 1990s, which led to a wonderful, warm, remarkable friendship that has endured for over 25 years. In addition, just a few weeks ago, I was honored to join 13 members of the football program on a Habitat for Humanity trip to Guatemala. It was an incredible experience—one that I will never, ever forget. What made it so special? It was the opportunity to do meaningful work away from campus with students. As a dean of students, one gets to see the good, the bad, and the ugly; it all has been and can be part of a rich, robust, and remarkable life.

Unfortunately, however, at some point in the late 1980s or maybe in the 1990s, things—life, the world—shifted, and relationships and the life of a dean of students became more complex; hugs and tough-love conversations were no longer appropriate responses. But I'm getting ahead of myself. It is first important to know the path to a dean of students' position.

When I Grow Up, I Want to Be a Dean

How many times have you asked yourself or been asked, "What do you want to be when you grow up?" Today, this question seems to create for students a higher level of angst than in years past. For me, until my last semester as an undergraduate student, the answer was "a doctor, either a surgeon or a psychiatrist." I applied to seven medical schools, and it was my seventh rejection letter that compelled me to change the answer to this question.

For whatever reason, I was not ready to give up completely my dream to be a physician. Although my grades were certainly less than subpar, I remained convinced that if given another chance, I could improve my GPA. I was able to talk my way into a master's program in health and hospital administration and did very well academically. Instead of reapplying to medical school, I decided to work for a few years. What a great decision that was, as I learned that the health-care environment was not for me. I decided after 18 months that I never wanted to work in health care again and that I was very grateful that the seven medical schools to which I had applied had rejected me. They knew me better than I did.

My work life at this point was miserable. I was certified to teach high school, but I was not truly interested in moving in that direction. While talking with friends in search of advice, I was reminded how much I loved being a resident assistant while in graduate school and was told about a student affairs position at my alma mater. Long story short, I applied, got the job as an administrative assistant working for the dean for student life, and knew within three days that this was the type of work I desired. It was a game changer, and I suddenly found my days being remarkably meaningful and fun.

The dean for whom I was working had oversight for student conduct, orientation, student disability services, parent programs, and Greek life. I found the student conduct work to be incredibly inspiring and Greek life both interesting and puzzling. As I had been a first-generation student on full financial aid, I had not experienced Greek life from the inside. Nevertheless, I did enjoy working with the student leaders within the Greek chapters, as they communicated openly with me and were committed to making their organizations better.

As luck would have it, the dean was offered an executive vice president position at another school and left within six months of my arrival. I was asked to just "keep the ship afloat" while they searched for his replacement. We were sued during this time, the search was delayed, and I kept the ship afloat for over six months. When the search finally opened, I decided to apply. Why not? I had nothing to lose and had found that in a very short period of time, I had come to love this work.

I was not the search committee's first choice; in fact, I came in third place. Again, lady luck was on my side, and the first 2 candidates declined the offer. Therefore, at the age of 25, with just a year's experience, I was suddenly a dean.

Knowledge and Skills Necessary for Being a Dean of Students (and How I Acquired and Learned Them)

No one ever really told me what to do and how to do it when I was appointed to the dean position. I was fortunate to be in a position to observe a number of different people and their styles of leadership and management, and I was able to see what I liked and what I did not like. I very quickly equated having effective relationships with students with being accessible and available to them. I found that administrators who made themselves available to students, particularly after hours, were the ones who had enviable relationships with students; it became quite obvious to me that students responded to and trusted the staff, even those in positions of authority, who showed they cared by spending time with them, even in the later hours of the day. I can vividly remember some amazing late-night conversations and debates with students in my office.

As a young professional who never imagined college administration as a career, it was quite enlightening for me to consider the academic backgrounds of student affairs administrators, particularly deans of students. When I first joined the profession, colleagues with divinity degrees or counseling backgrounds were prevalent, so I was not certain if my master's in health and hospital administration was going to be at all relevant or helpful. What I found was that virtually any advanced degree was advantageous, as the actual area of study was not as important as the process of getting the degree. Furthermore, I decided during my first five years as a dean of students that it would be in my best interest to pursue a terminal degree. Again, my sense was that the actual degree was not as important as getting the degree, so I looked at three possibilities: a doctorate in education, a law degree, and a doctorate in business. I talked with faculty and attended classes in all three disciplines, trying to decide which would give me the most flexibility while being the most enjoyable and stimulating from an academic standpoint. I really wanted to enjoy getting the degree and learn as much as I could. In the end, I decided to pursue a law degree and applied to the only part-time program in my area.

I was lucky enough to get into law school and ended up liking it so much that I pursued an advanced law degree and then practiced law for nine months. As much as I liked studying the law and respected my colleagues in the law firm that hired me, I realized very quickly that I missed my work with students. Fortunately, I had taken a leave of absence from my dean of students' role, and the vice president of student affairs at the time told me she would "leave the light on" for me. In addition, I had maintained contact with many students and continued to advise several student organizations while I was practicing law. Therefore, once again, lady luck was with me, and I was able to return to the university where I had worked. As it turned out, I sometimes think that the best preparation I received to be a dean of students was a law degree, and I will always encourage student affairs professionals to consider law school.

Things Just Aren't Like They Used to Be

There was something magical about being a dean of students in the 1980s. Of course, there were concerns about hazing, students making poor choices, plagiarizing, and plenty of emergencies, just like today. Students struggling with eating disorders had begun to get more attention, and the legal and ethical expectation that colleges and universities provide access and support to students with disabilities began to emerge in earnest.

So, what was so different? Well, for one thing, I was much younger. Many days, I felt too young, so much so that I worried that parents and students looked at me and wondered if I knew anything! Fortunately (or unfortunately), I have always looked older than I am.

One issue that has remained significant is alcohol. I vividly remember as a freshman during orientation week in the early 1970s attending "The Happening" on the quad at my alma mater, where over 40 kegs of beer were available to all students, regardless of age. Similarly, as an undergrad, I could go to the fraternity section in the neighboring residence hall, put a quarter in the vending machine, and get a Coke, a Sprite, or a Budweiser. Can you imagine this today on any college campus?

By the 1980s, Mothers Against Drunk Driving (MADD) emerged as one of the national organizations to have a major impact on campus life. Since MADD successfully advocated to raise the age to consume alcohol to 21 years, campuses across the country have continued to struggle with ways to enforce this law. For many campuses, the emphasis over the years has been on preventing abusive consumption of alcohol and promoting safety instead of focusing on underage drinking. Unfortunately, we have struggled to communicate this goal to students, as they still think that our priority is cracking down on underage consumption. I can remember walking into a student party and having students jump out of windows, just to avoid getting caught drinking underage.

The past 3 to 4 decades have continued to be challenging, as deans of students have tried to balance the need to enforce the law and to keep students safe. There was a time when I thought it would be best to return to a drinking age of 18 years for beer and wine. However, it may be that we waited too long to consider this shift, as the notion of pregaming (consuming alcohol before an actual event) is such a significant component of today's college culture.

The other complication that did not exist in the 1980s, certainly not to the extent as it does today, is the role that parents play in their college students' lives. With many parents shielding their children from failure and disappointment, current students seem to be less resilient. This generation reports more stress, anxiety, and depression, along with other mental health challenges, than prior generations, and my experience as a dean of students certainly aligns with these data (Hoff, 2018; Perry, 2018).

Dealing with involved parents has become a skill that is required of any dean of students and, for that matter, any student affairs professional. Having started in this profession just five years after the Family Education Rights to Privacy Act (FERPA) was passed, it has been difficult for me to understand how parents today have approached their student's college experience. Having gone to college on the heels of students demanding independence from their parents, I have found the recent shift to a form of *in loco parentis* challenging.

From the late 1970s through the early 2000s, the notion of a college or university stepping into the shoes of parents and playing somewhat of a parental role became very unpopular. While the millennial student has been shown to have a close and positive relationship with parents, this relationship sometimes manifests itself in parents contacting the college whenever their son or daughter fails to respond to a text. The definition of an *emergency* has certainly changed, and it has placed undue stress on the student affairs professionals who never imagined they would be expected to track down a 20-year-old and ask the student to call home. Furthermore, I cannot help but think about how many times I hear that "we" applied to college and "we" are trying to decide on a major and "we" need to make a doctor's appointment. No wonder many of today's students fall far short of expressing significant independence of any kind from their parents.

Regardless, a dean of students must be able to interact with parents on a very regular basis and be willing to patiently listen and respond to their concerns while also encouraging them to allow their college students to take responsibility for their lives. Frankly, I have always enjoyed working with parents, particularly alumni parents whom I knew when they were students. I love to threaten, in jest, to share their disciplinary records with their children!

Living, Literally, With Freshmen and Feeling Their Joy and Pain

Five years ago, I moved into a residence hall of almost 200 first-year students. This position of faculty-in-residence gives students an opportunity to interact with a faculty member on a daily basis with the hope of experiencing faculty as inspiring yet approachable scholars. In other words, they learn that faculty are human, just like everyone else!

For me, as a dean of students, the chance to live with students has provided a unique and enormously insightful window into the approach that today's students take to college. I have such a better understanding of their preparation for college, their expectations, their relationships with their parents, their study habits, their sleep habits, their friendships, their use of technology, their views on alcohol and drugs and sex, and their hopes for the future. I am particularly mindful of the stress, anxiety, and other mental health challenges that today's students experience.

The stress is real and so is the anxiety. I am not sure where it all comes from and why it is significantly more intense than it was even 10 years ago, but I do know that it is authentic. The students feel it, and they are willing to acknowledge it and talk about it. I have learned that any attempt to minimize the worries and concerns that students are feeling is not only inappropriate but also hurtful and minimizes their experience. Telling a student to "get a grip" or "suck it up" and then giving that student a hug may be detrimental as well as inappropriate.

I do not mean to be dramatic or trivialize what students are feeling today; instead, I am trying to bring as much validity as I can to where the mental state of college students is today. With this in mind, it is important for colleges and universities to focus on teaching students how to cope with stress and become more resilient. As a dean of students, I have chosen to learn mindfulness mediation and teach it to students. In addition, I continue to focus on being a better listener, recognizing that many students and staff just need someone with whom to share their worries, particularly their anxieties related to the future.

What about other potential sources of stress that students feel? Might it be their parents and the need for them to protect their children from anything that could compromise their safety or their ability to succeed? Does the stress come from a fear of failure, or is it from the fear of missing out? Is it a result of technology and this generation's ability and need to always be connected? Is it perhaps a fear of not being as successful as their parents? Alternatively, maybe it is all the tragedies they have witnessed, such as 9/11 and school shootings? They have had so many opportunities to view the world as a very scary place.

Regardless of the origin of this stress and anxiety, these conditions are real, challenging, and pervasive. That being said, I love living with these students and find the experience to be inspiring and fun; they bring a special meaning to being a dean of students. So, if you ever have a chance to live with students in a residence hall, do it! I promise you will not regret it.

Call Me, Maybe? No, Just Text Me

Speaking of stress and other mental health concerns, it is important to take a closer look at the impact of technology on being a dean of students. A new term, *nomophobia*, has been proposed to define the fear of being out of cellular phone contact (Elmore, 2014). I have certainly experienced this fear myself, especially in my role as dean of students, as the thought of not being able to be reached (or to reach others) causes me great angst. I can only imagine how our students must feel, as they have always been connected to everyone and everything whenever they want to be, having instant access to information and other people.

Yet the impact of always being connected is not necessarily positive; in fact, it is downright unhealthy. These days, it seems that everyone is always connected, and the expectation is that we, as deans of students (and our staffs), be able to respond immediately every time we are contacted. This has become a common standard that is hard to meet.

How are we to deal with such connectivity that is clearly affecting the well-being of our students as well as our own? The answers, unfortunately, are not clear, as the technology genie is completely out of the bottle and is not going back in. We cannot ignore the impact of social media on our students and on all that we do, as we have very little, if any, time to think, process, reflect, consult, or react before whatever we have said or done is shared and gone viral on social media. There is no longer any opportunity to change one's response or to ask for forgiveness—it will always be too little, too late!

In many ways, our students and younger colleagues understand this impact of technology better than we do, and as hard as I have tried to adjust, I continue to be amazed and distressed by the power of social media. Whether the story is accurate or not, once it is out there, it is the story that everyone believes and embraces, and no one ever considers the notion that the version he or she is seeing might be incorrect or fake news.

This particular lack of forgiveness is even more evident today on college campuses with issues related to freedom of speech and diversity. Although freedom of speech has been debated on college campuses for decades, it appears to have taken on an even more elevated level of significance most recently, as controversial speakers are finding their way to campuses and students are expressing their dissatisfaction with these speakers.

What does free speech mean today, particularly in light of our more diverse campus? If speech makes one uncomfortable or unsafe or creates a feeling of harassment, should the college permit it? As with the issue of sexual misconduct, deans of students find themselves right in the middle of these disputes, expected to reconcile speech policies and student protesters and community standards.

The notion of civilized discourse seems, unfortunately, to be something that people either do not want to engage in or lack the ability to do. Many of the students of today do not even want to talk on the phone, let alone have a one-on-one, face-to-face dialogue. How did this happen, and what might be the long-term effects?

For many decades, college administrators, and deans of students in particular, have been able to be effective in their roles because of their relationships with students, and these relationships have been affected by the power of the human voice. Today, with students and younger colleagues preferring to communicate through texts and e-mails and social media, the value gained by hearing the human voice is being quickly lost, and our students' ability to work through conflict is being compromised.

Unfortunately, this move to electronic communication is not limited to the college campus, so our students are being influenced by many role models at home and in the corporate and political worlds. I think we need to do all we can to resist this inclination, even though it feels like a losing proposition.

This lack of human connection is not the only adverse impact emanating from technology. As previously mentioned, the need to be connected 24/7 has had a major effect on our ability to be and stay in the present. With so many distractions, our thoughts and the thoughts of our students continue to be all over the place as we struggle to maintain a focus on the here and now. Whether it's thoughts of worry, anxiety, stress, or the future, our minds wander, and if we have a moment to relax and reflect, we tend to fill it with a glance at our smartphone.

Moreover, whatever adventure or experience our students may be having, it is not complete unless they share a picture on social media. In spite of the fact that our students are more inclined to wear their seat belts in a car and a helmet when on a bike, our students find it extremely difficult to take time to reflect and be mindful. In addition, it is not just our students but us as well—their deans of students and other administrators—who struggle to stay focused, be in the present, reflect, and slow down.

Given all the demands on deans of students today, one of the most critical things that we can do is take care of ourselves, including taking the time to rest and relax. Even more important, we need to model what we want our students to do, and that includes getting sufficient sleep. Constantly talking about how busy we are and taking pride in calendars that are completely filled is not what our students need to hear from us. Instead, we need to commit to our own personal wellness and practice and model self-care. This is likely to be difficult for many of us as our sense of being responsible and accountable takes over. But it is absolutely necessary to do this job over the long haul and set a positive example for students to follow.

If You Want to Become a Dean of Students, Consider This

Perhaps the next generations of deans of students need to rethink the role that they play in creating the various boundary-less expectations they communicate to students and their parents. As we have heard many college admissions pitches and reviewed numerous university websites, it seems we are all marketing ourselves as being everything to everybody all of the time. Is it possible that we have created this monster ourselves by promising to always be available? Somehow, we need to creatively figure out a new way to effectively deliver our services because what we are currently doing is not sustainable.

Much of what has been modeled for me during my career has been to do whatever it takes to get the job done, and that is how I have handled my responsibilities. I vividly remember a conversation that I had with the first vice president for student affairs to whom I reported (I have always adored and respected him—he was and is an incredible role model). It was quite early in my career, and he advised me to take time away from work and enjoy my personal life. He shared his regrets for not having approached his career in this way and steered me in the direction of work–life balance. I heard what he said and clearly have not forgotten it, but I have certainly never practiced it.

As indicated previously, it is my strong belief that one's effectiveness as a dean of students on any campus is directly related to the relationships one has been able to cultivate, but not just with students or colleagues within student affairs. Whether it is the folks in academic affairs, athletics, development, alumni affairs, admissions, housekeeping, or parking, the dean of students needs to know everyone.

However, at the end of the day, one of the most important things to consider when thinking about becoming a dean of students is related to the many and ongoing demands that the position presents. Whether in the 1980s or today, the dean of students' position can be an all-encompassing one, as serving as a dean of students is not a job but a way of life. I have clearly not been able to set boundaries for myself in an effective way over the years and have failed at achieving work–life balance. Though I've never really tried to find that balance, I've instead looked to create more of a work–life integration, attempting to not separate my work from my personal life but weave them together in such a way that I can get my work done and have fun. I do not need a separation between work and students, so the dean of students' role has worked well for me. In addition, such a position highlights the various synergies that exist between people, relationships, events, and activities whether related to work or to play.

To me, it is more about creating a life that provides energy, joy, and relevance. With such an approach, the separation of professional and personal goals became less necessary for me (although some would certainly disagree with this, as I was divorced after 20 years of marriage). I have just as much, if not more, fun going to a performance on campus with students than with friends. After all, you had better love doing things with students if you truly want to be a successful and content dean of students.

Though I have been slightly better in my later years, this notion of balance has never truly resonated with me, yet I emphasize it to our students on a daily basis. Many of my younger colleagues have called me out for preaching wellness but not modeling it through my approach to work. Of course, they are right—at least for them, as we may all have a different yet successful way of approaching the responsibilities of a dean of students' position. What I do advise is that young professionals give thought to what is important to them and how they want to organize their work life and personal life, because there are many ways to create balance or integration. There will be times when the demands presented by a dean of students' position are overwhelming and all-encompassing, and personal life may need to take a back seat, hopefully for just a while. That is just an inescapable reality.

In addition, the need to be nimble and flexible is critical. Deans of students are normally responsible for responding to critical incidents, whether it be a residence hall fire, a student suicide, an accident in which a student has been involved, a campus demonstration or protest, or any other crisis. Because these situations cannot be scheduled and are rarely possible to anticipate, deans of students (and their staffs) must be ready to literally drop whatever it is they are doing and make their way to campus immediately. Do not ever throw away your ticket to a movie, as you might need to leave and return later (even another day) to view the part of the movie you missed. It's happened to me more than once—just show the ticket to the box office folks and explain to them what happened. It's worked for me every time!

Therefore, in the final analysis, there are many, many ways to *be* a dean of students and *do* all that the position requires. For me, I was able to approach it in a way that worked for me, and I was able to do so by remaining on the same campus for my entire career in higher education. What might work for you?

My Advice for the Next Deans of Students

As retirement for me is on the horizon, I think more about the next generation of student affairs professionals and the role that the dean of students will play. It is hard to predict what a dean of students might need to prepare to be and do, but there are a few things that appear to be evident.

- Technology will continue to be a significant part of life in higher education. Keeping up with new devices, new software, new social media, and even new video games will be critical, as all of this will be influencing the lives of the students, and the dean of students should be able to understand these influences.
- Given that an understanding of budgets, personnel management, and legal liability will continue to be a requirement for those in leadership positions in higher education, it may be propitious for those aspiring to be a dean of students to review their skills and preparation in these areas.

- Cultivate a multifaceted skill set. The role of a dean of students requires us to work with the mind-set of a generalist; we must be able to respond to issues in different areas while always having a global view integrating other areas of the institution. Having an interest in and understanding of literally all aspects of higher education is crucial.
- If making a lot of money and having significant privacy and personal space is required in one's life, then being a dean of students may not be a good choice. However, a dean of students can live almost anywhere in the world, select an environment and climate that is personally suitable, and find an institution that capitalizes on strengths and aligns with personal values.

As I finish writing this chapter, I am sitting on a plane accompanying a colleague from the development office to meet with alumni and donors. Over these next few days, I will have a chance to meet and interact with alumni whom I may have known when they were students; with parents of current and past students; and with current new students, some of whom will be living in my residence hall. My mind will be flooded with memories of decades gone by and with eager anticipation of the year ahead.

In so many ways, I have led a charmed life, and I wish for anyone reading this book that you, too, can discover, *in your own way*, what I have experienced as a dean of students. I hope in reading this chapter you have felt my passion for the work that I have had the privilege of doing over the past 40 years. Being a dean of students and living in a freshman residence hall has been spectacular, and I only hope that you have a chance to experience the joy that I have felt over the years. I never considered being a college administrator, but I will be forever grateful for this opportunity.

References

Elmore, T. (2014). Nomophobia: A rising trend in students. Retrieved from https://www.psychologytoday.com/us/blog/artificial-maturity/201409/nomophobia-rising-trend-in-students

Hoff, V. (2018, May 30). Our state of mind: 13 important statistics about millennials and mental health. *The Thirty*. Retrieved from https://thethirty.byrdie.com/millennial-mental-health-statistics--5b082b0a1de14

Perry, P. (2018, January 8). Millennials are at a higher risk for mental health issues. This may be why. *Big Think*. Retrieved from https://bigthink.com/philip-perry/millennials-are-at-higher-risk-for-mental-health-issues-this-may-be-why

9

THE DEAN OF STUDENTS
IN RETROSPECT
AND PROSPECT

James J. Rhatigan and James W. Lyons

hat can two former administrators, now in their eighties, contribute to a discussion about the challenges of current deans of students? During our tenure, we did not have e-mail, smartphones or even cell phones, personal computers, texting, Facebook, Instagram, Snapchat, Twitter, Skype, or wireless devices of any kind. We do not recall that the cyber world was even a topic of discussion on the college campus. The word *website* did not appear in the dictionary.

As we pondered the invitation to consider the dean of students' position in retrospect, we thought the first and most obvious issue would be bridging the gap between our years of work. Perhaps it would help, in our view, for the modern dean to look at some of our issues.

The 1960s were years of substantial growth in the student affairs field. Some of that was positive, but some of it was in response to crisis. Until 1964, there was little evidence of dramatic national issues affecting college campuses in the United States. The assassination of President Kennedy clearly changed that, influencing higher education in the years that would follow. Many would argue that the impact of this death was a seminal event, quietly influencing the mood of our country for many years. In 1968, Martin Luther King Jr. was assassinated, and a few weeks later, Robert Kennedy was as well.

The most immediate and volatile issue of those years was the growing military conflict in Vietnam. This was not a remote matter; the military draft was deeply concerning. As the undeclared war deepened, the campus response from students grew in scope and intensity. Often students were joined by faculty and staff sympathetic to their views. Campus violence increased throughout the country. During this period, the Twenty-Sixth Amendment was passed, lowering the voting age to 18 years. This made students full citizens with the rights and privileges of all other citizens. It accelerated the demise of *in loco parentis* (i.e., the college acting in lieu of parents), which was replaced by the law.

A corollary issue, today identified as the "free speech" movement, initially surfaced on campuses on both coasts, soon spreading nationwide, creating problems that deans of students were expected to manage. Previous "time, manner, and place" rules governing speech were challenged and occasionally fell by the wayside.

Another issue became acute racial injustice, beginning off campus but soon appearing directly on the campus. In a brief period of time in 1967, the word *Negro*, which had for decades been used to identify people of color, became something akin to a hate word. This began in California but spread rapidly. Students rallied to be identified as *Black*, and with this new insistence, previously unrealized anger and substantive issues came into the open.

After the publication of Betty Friedan's (1963) book *The Feminine Mystique*, women's voices became more public and insistent, adding to the issues of campus concern. This was just the onset of what would occur in a more organized and persuasive form a decade later, but initial activists were visible indeed in the 1960s.

The campus also had to deal with a drug culture of greater significance than previously experienced in American history (other than alcohol). While marijuana was the major drug of choice, more destructive drugs also found their way into the campus culture. This resulted in more law enforcement interest in campus life, a presence that has grown and spread to other issues.

Issues that would intensify later required attention, including the concerns of Hispanic students. Gay and lesbian students were present on campus, but in those days they were heavily marginalized. They focused on safety matters and sought space on campus where they could be ensured privacy. Students with disabilities were small in number but a growing population throughout the 1960s. Accessibility on many campuses was poor, and enthusiasm for addressing issues raised by students was modest at best. The political clout of this group continued, culminating in the Americans with Disabilities Act of 1990.

Somewhere in this roiling mix, deans of students had to deal with usual student issues, including students who were rebelling against their parents, those experiencing loneliness and depression, and the other less defined but still serious issues of the day.

Student affairs programs were in the middle of these concerns, made difficult because old rules no longer applied. In some parts of the country, "control" of situations was more important to presidents and governing boards than the underlying substantive issues that created them. For many months in the 1960s, the word *planning* meant planning for the day ahead.

The nature and speed of communication available now is indeed mindboggling, even numbing. How many times in a day does a dean of students have to say during a conversation, "Excuse me, I have to take this call"? The content issues of our work seem similar, but the stress we felt is more challenging for contemporary deans, because access to information and communication is almost instantaneous. It is clear that the inescapable character of instant communication is . . . inescapable. Eventually this will exact a cost.

That "call one has to take" may add to the burden of a day, not subtract from it—an excellent example of how constant accessibility produces stress. It may well be that conversations need to take place between an institution's expectations of its deans and the deans' expectations of their institution. A disconnect of any major sort can result in serious consequences, including in regard to one's mental and physical well-being. It appears to us that connectivity resulting from speed may at times be a deterrent to effective communication. In fact, it could be argued that communication without time for reflection is a curse.

Core Beliefs

In 1937, a remarkable document was prepared by a number of our pioneers. Esther Lloyd-Jones is regarded as the principal writer, though a number of outstanding practitioners and faculty contributed on a committee commissioned by the American Council on Education (ACE). The result was *The Student Personnel Point of View* (ACE, 1937). It conveyed for the first time in a written document a number of beliefs and assumptions that were held to be of principal importance in working with students. The document was revisited in 1949 by the ACE Committee on Student Personnel Work, not so much to displace any of the earlier writing but to add observations following World War II, including education for democracy, for international understanding, and to better address and solve social problems.

In 1987, we were a part of a group called the New Century Committee, a group commissioned by the NASPA–Student Affairs Administrators in Higher Education president Judy Chambers and led by Art Sandeen. Chambers believed that a reexamination of *The Student Personnel Point of View* would be a worthwhile effort. With the growing diversity of students, the exploding number and types of campuses, and the different kinds of services and developmental opportunities afforded to students, how did the original thinking of our predecessors hold up? Quite well, it turned out. The New Century Committee members scrutinized the 1937 statement line by line, sentence by sentence, and when *A Perspective on Student Affairs* (NASPA, 1987) was written, there were no unexpected findings. The committee offered a modern emphasis but an underlying confirmation of their brilliant work.

We are writing in 2018, some 30-plus years later. Given the technological revolution in the intervening years, what professional core beliefs for deans of students seem to be enduring? Here are an important few.

Embrace the academic mission. We believe that if one aspires to be a successful dean of students, that person should understand and then embrace the academic mission of the institution. At first glance, this seems like the primary domain of faculty. Of course, it is, but they do not own it exclusively. We taught in ways of our devising, sometimes in the classroom but more often outside to serve and enrich the cause of teaching and the development of a variety of life skills. We wanted to help craft a community where reason, intellectual effort, curiosity, and civility were in the forefront of the campus culture. We were committed to the idea that citizenship can be taught. Certainly, we did not see ourselves on the sidelines or in secondary service. We felt that we were an integral part of teaching and learning as part of the institution's academic mission.

In the intervening years, a group of distinguished scholars from NASPA and the American College Personnel Association (ACPA) prepared *Learning Reconsidered*, providing depth to the core beliefs of the best who came before (Keeling, 2004). The writers of that work understood the value of learning communities within the general campus and the need for academic partnerships throughout the campus. They reinforced the idea that a transformative education relies on an effective implementation of the academic mission of the campus.

Individuals differ. While the academic mission is always primary, it is not the only mission. In varying ways, the question "Who am I?" has always been a matter of importance that students needed help to answer. The question is quietly resolved by many students, but for others it is a matter of such consequence that their progress may be threatened without facing and addressing it. Economic status, appearance, race, ethnicity, gender, sexual preference, language, dress style, religion, and family history are examples. The answer to "Who am I?" usually does not present itself as just one of these examples but will appear in combination. One of our most important obligations was to create a campus environment free from these limiting shackles. We frequently came up short, yet to admit we could not do everything does not mean that we could not do anything. How we judge others, and the impact of that judgment, is an issue that will always be with us. For each new generation, an accepting campus will mitigate the problem of individual identity.

The need for deans to be active learners. The best among us were active learners, people who thought about, wrote, taught, and shared their views. They had a good sense of the components of a campus environment and how it could be influenced, developed, or injured. We believe the prevailing attitude was anthropomorphic, seeing the campus as a living thing. The best deans in those days were students of students, development, culture, and conflict; they tried diligently to understand and share understanding of the powerful interactions of environment and behavior.

The unending search for community. The idea of community often is a description used more as nostalgia than reality. Administrative silos long have been metaphors in opposition to community, and this was true in our day. Even students often took narrow views that centered on their concerns, with no energy left for issues beyond their own. The best deans of students in those days continued to use their administrative roles to teach honesty, fairness, civility, and social justice. We believe they helped guide our educational institutions through some very perilous times. We understand that community is an elusive ideal, but the very power of the idea will always be worth pursuing.

Effective citizenship can be taught, must be taught. Citizenship is complex, but there is no better way to introduce it than on the campus. Active participation in the routine matters of institutional governance, community service, and collective management of students' own affairs is key to responsible citizenship. This core value required overt teaching by the dean of students. Others contributed, but we assert that in our time it was one of our most important undertakings. Citizenship mechanisms provided frameworks from which the freedom to doubt and question were ensured. It provided opportunities for discussions on solutions or at least how situations could be made better. Successful citizenship was not a matter of decoration but a basis for students' understanding that in the larger world they were about to enter, cooperation and collaboration would be needed in their communities.

Students are responsible for their own lives. The campus is not a therapeutic milieu; it can be competitive, insensitive, and hostile. Out-of-class environments are rarely neutral; they help or detract from the student experience (NASPA, 1987). This is why the extra curriculum looms large. Students must gain the confidence to direct their own thinking. Through active participation they will be better able to see how the life they desire for themselves is wrapped up in the aspirations of other lives. With the proper knowledge and assistance, students almost always make good choices. Very readily, they become teachers. The dean of students should be a part of this process, providing space, financial support, advice, experience, and mature judgment.

Best and Worst Practices

By necessity, student affairs grew from the bottom up. There was no literature on which our pioneers could rely. A principal tool in effective work in those days was observing the good work of others, whether on campus or across the nation. Early deans were storytellers, and important lessons were embedded in those stories. This teaching function still exists in student affairs, as one learns in visiting with colleagues or attending meetings. "Best practices" exist, but very seldom do you find them in a written compilation; more likely, they will occur as anecdotes or stories (Rhatigan, 2000).

We decided that in the brief sections that follow, we would write exclusively in the first person. We know that at the receiving end of our words, there is a reader who is a dean of students or someone aspiring to be one. We want you to see more of the common, day-to-day practices we did or observed, because you will be able to recognize how they square with your own perceptions and experiences. We believe reputations develop from these practices. If you are just thinking about the position of dean of students, our comments may help you make a solid beginning.

Best Practices

Write four notes a day. Effective administrators quickly determine the limits of the bureaucratic power they possess. To do the work they desire, successful deans will seek to use other power sources, as in "the power of influence," available to them. This requires creativity, and perhaps no textbook is available to illustrate what might be done. We believe one way is to write personal notes.

If you were to write 4 personal notes a day (Monday through Friday), as an example both of us practiced, you would reach 1,000 people a year, 10,000 people in a decade. These notes need meet only the following criteria: (a) Every note must be original, (b) every note must be deserved, and (c) every note must be brief (or we would not write them). A first reaction might be skepticism; who has the kind of free time to write notes? In fact, writing them rarely took more than 10 or 15 minutes a day.

We do not have to speculate on the outcomes of this disciplined effort. We regard them as extraordinary, an investment producing returns beyond any expectation. In these notes you will affirm others, congratulate or sympathize with them, or express appreciation or concern across a variety of issues. (There is no limit on the topic you choose to write about.) You will hear from the recipients, directly or indirectly, many of them completely surprised and uniformly appreciative. They may see a side of you of which they were unaware. Relationships developed from these notes, and/or previous perceptions were altered. It was apparent that the messages often were shared with others; those ensuing connections could be seen as a multiplier effect.

Initiate faculty and staff contacts. One of our colleagues decided each fall semester to personally reach out to every new member of the faculty. This number was often in the range of 40 to 50 a year. He went to their offices, explained how student affairs might be useful to them from time to time, and offered to help on issues whenever they might feel it useful. In just a few years, he knew hundreds of faculty. Professional staff should not be neglected; it could be argued that departmental secretaries (as they were called then) often served as frontline supporters of student affairs when they were well informed.

Small wins. We define a *small win* as any behavior that leads to a positive outcome. You employ small wins every day, but many people fail to notice the power they possess. Sometimes in administrative life a small win may seem relatively unimportant, but a series of small wins in addressing difficult issues can help reduce the feeling that they are almost incapable of solution. It is important to see how, when issues are recast, they may seem less forbidding and more approachable.

Small wins not only are incidental but also should be employed as a purposeful and integral part of work. They are useful because they tend to be more understandable, doable, nonthreatening, and repeatable. They can produce results that never could have been anticipated at the beginning.

Small wins are particularly useful in dealing with individual student issues. A student might bring to the office a sense of malaise that really is just a matter of not seeing things clearly. Sometimes things seem to be very complicated, but when the parts are identified, their resolution might give a student encouragement. Student affairs professionals always have indicated an interest in the "whole student," but students tend to appear at a particular moment with a specific obstacle or issue they need help to resolve. Helping in that moment might be both a small win for you and a huge assistance for them.

Visit other campuses. Much can be learned from visiting other campuses to observe how colleagues handle opening days, orientation, recruiting, staff training, or any number of issues. If a neighboring campus is within reasonable distance, going there is a learning opportunity. It would be unusual to find a dean who would not welcome you. Take as many of your staff as you can. It is an inexpensive opportunity to observe, learn, and possibly make suggestions that will be useful to your host. A visit may assure you that you are employing good practices at home, and it did not require a paid consultant! Make such visits reciprocal.

The press. Develop a relationship with the press. On large campuses, the responsibility with the public press officially rests with large staffs outside student affairs, but there is always a way you can establish a relationship with a reporter who will appreciate background information that may provide nuance to a story. Establishing trust is an investment worth making, and trust is in need of protecting.

Of course, all campuses have a newspaper. It is in your best interest to have an open, accessible relationship with the editor and staff writers. When the press is honored, good things can happen. Even when the news is bad, basic relationships that have been built can make it less bad. One cannot wait for a crisis to develop a relationship.

It is somewhat amazing to observe how apprehensive colleagues can be of the press. Every year, if you have a large enough staff, they should be afforded a training workshop opportunity that explains "what to do when the press calls." Oh yes, be sure to include the press in that workshop!

Periodically, we dropped by the paper, showed interest, which indicated our availability. Always return calls to the staff with their deadlines in mind. Consider providing your home or cell number. Answer questions whenever possible. If you are limited in your ability to respond or are proscribed from answering, try to get the newspaper staff to the proper source.

Of primary importance, remember that the campus press is composed of students. They are all in a learning mode and will make mistakes. Every year (or so) there is a new group. Help them be better in every possible way. Your reputation will very likely be transmitted over time among the news staff.

Understanding national symbols. A good practice, here, is for the campus to have a sound, well-understood position when free speech and the perceived abuse of national symbols are in conflict. Examples from our era centered on the flag, and today it might be kneeling during the national anthem. The dean of students can expect to be in the middle of controversies of this sort. We believe this is an area where a campus crisis team must permanently be in place that can be called into action. If you are not part of it, you should offer to be of help. You need to be involved because very likely you are going to be on the front line of campus responders.

The perceived misuse of one our national symbols is one among only a few issues that will call out the president. Every incident is different, but the campus must be prepared to respond, because the repercussions may envelop the campus. In these difficult situations, a considered response is an institution's best protection. Any campus that has paid attention to this issue in advance is more likely to survive intact.

Listening intensely. The best deans among us were intense listeners. They understood that listening was not a passive exercise but part of a transaction. They made better connections with students because they heard more. Students may not be precise, but they provide clues from which we can look deeper. This enriches responses. Many times, it is possible to start preparing an answer to an issue before a student has even finished stating it. Tempting as this may be, best practices are aligned with an open mind and good listening.

Worst Practices

During our years of work, colleagues rose and fell for a variety of reasons. Worst practices accounted greatly for the latter outcome. Deans who failed did not understand the consequences of their behaviors, even though friends and colleagues may have offered their suggestions or warnings. The following sections describe some of the more grievous of these practices. Few deans can survive them, and along the way other staff will suffer from them.

The inability to admit error. Goofs happen. Admit it. The inability to admit error is an ego issue. Its consequences will cause pain for everyone within the dean's sphere of responsibility. A dogmatic dean cannot be effectively confronted or educated, and staff who try may well get run over.

Underpreparation. Effective administration is characterized by good preparation by people who have thought out the positions they hold. There were in our day, however, a number of highly intelligent colleagues who often got by for periods of time through "winging it." People who underprepare eventually will be identified and discounted by colleagues throughout the institution.

Self-promotion. Imperiousness rarely works. Some colleagues will look toward their next promotion before they address the problems in their current assignment. The worst examples reveal deans who take credit for the work of others or fail to express appreciation and who love status more than relationships. They do not inspire and generally do not earn loyalty or trust.

Play favorites. Playing favorites may be a matter of both perception and practice. It is understandable that some colleagues are more enjoyable than others are, but inclusivity needs to be an imperative for a dean. We *all* want to be part of a thriving, prospering team.

Lack of warmth. Because institutions are organized hierarchically, some deans respond accordingly. They fail to express concern or understand the important issues in other people's lives. Staff joys, birthdays, children's achievements, and similar issues do not seem to be a matter of interest. We regard any goodwill that is passed by as a self-inflicted wound.

Seem overworked. Some deans of students seem to love to proclaim how hard they work. Certainly, deans should set an example, but all good colleagues work hard and want to be appreciated for their efforts. The dean who suggests fatigue from work will not be admired but may be viewed by staff as inadequate and unable to do the work at hand.

Failure to focus. A particular day may bring stresses and worries from home or trouble with a colleague somewhere on campus—wearisome distractions that are understandable. It can affect our focus. Students may sense this but will not understand it. It may just affirm for them that their issues are not that important. Don't look for them to return. What if this were a day, a time, and an opportunity when you could have made a difference in a life?

Looking Forward

We subscribe to the adage that to live is to change, but we also believe that change can be influenced. That is the very basis of our work. Knowledge from an earlier day will always be relevant in some way, because our work is part of the human venture. It will in its own way endure, and it becomes part of our story. A dedicated life has many aspects, but work is one of the most important of them. The more intelligently we approach it, the better we will look back on it with satisfaction. It will be true that we do not always know how all the things we did worked out. This is not our destiny.

We cannot know the pressures your future portends. It seems likely, though, that issues of importance to your life and work will be only partially answered by new knowledge. Core beliefs will be both a respite and a guide, continuing to offer you moral sensitivity and an adherence to principle.

A fortunate reader one day will reach the old age of the authors. We hope that you will be provided the opportunity that has come our way, to reflect on what you have learned in the hope that parts of it will be useful to others.

Editors' Note

We are sad to share that on February 9, 2019, Jim W. Lyons, coauthor of this chapter, passed away. He will long be remembered by his family, friends, colleagues, and former students, and we are grateful for the wisdom and experience he shared in this chapter.

References

American Council on Education. (1937). *The student personnel point of view* (American Council on Education Studies, Series 1, No. 3). Washington, DC: Author.

American Council on Education, Committee on Student Personnel Work. (1949). *The student personnel point of view* (Rev. ed., American Council on Education Studies, Series 6, No. 13). Washington, DC: Author.

Friedan, B. (1963). *The feminine mystique*. New York, NY: W. W. Norton.

Keeling, R. P. (2004). *Learning reconsidered: A campus-wide focus on the student experience*. Washington, DC: National Association of Student Personnel Administrators and American College Personnel Association.

National Association of Student Personnel Administrators. (1987). *A perspective on student affairs*. Washington, DC: Author.

Rhatigan, J. J. (2000). The history and philosophy of student affairs. In M. J. Barr & M. K. Desler (Eds.), *The handbook of student affairs administration* (pp. 6–24). San Francisco, CA: Jossey-Bass.

References

10

THE ESSENCE OF BEING
A DEAN OF STUDENTS

Lori S. White

This book provides both historical and contemporary perspectives on the role of the dean of students on college campuses. A takeaway from the preceding chapters is that the role of the dean of students is complex in terms of the issues a dean may face and that the scope and focus of the role may be different depending on the institutional context.

Prior to becoming a vice president (or vice chancellor) for student affairs (VPSA), I served as a dean of students, and I have also supervised deans of students in my senior student affairs officer role. In a recent online conversation with some of my VPSA colleagues, we had a robust discussion around what we thought the essence of a dean of students to be. In the course of our e-mail exchanges also raised was the question of whether the need for the dean of students' title and/or role still exists—a question, among others related to the essence of being a dean of students, I explore in this closing chapter.

As the author of this chapter, let me provide some of my background. I have enjoyed an almost 40-year-long career in student affairs, and like many of my VPSA colleagues, I worked my way up through various student affairs roles as coordinator, director, assistant dean, assistant/associate vice president (AVP), and dean of students to the VPSA. As the VPSA, I oversee a complex organization with many different departments, manage a multimillion-dollar budget, participate at the highest levels of university decision-making, and am the chief advocate and voice for student concerns "in the room where it happens." In the hours of a single day, I can be asked to engage in strategic planning, crisis management, mentoring of staff, meetings with student leaders, fund-raising and development, and all of the other things—planned and unplanned—that constitute a daily VPSA schedule. Over the course of my career, I have seen the issues and challenges faced by students become ever more complex. This has been accompanied by rising expectations from students, parents, alumni, boards of trustees, state legislators, the federal government, and other stakeholders as to the types of higher education services, programs, and responses to various issues our institutions, often student affairs specifically, should (or should not) provide. I share the aforementioned to provide some context for my reflections in this chapter.

Let me begin with some retrospection. As I sat down to write my contribution to this book on the role of the dean of students, I reviewed the book *Pieces of Eight: The Rites, Roles, and Styles of the Dean, by Eight Who Have Been There* (Appleton, 1978). This text describes the roles and challenges of deans of students during the era in which the book was written and provides advice to the reader about the skills and abilities for successful *deaning*. While reading the book, I thought of how the book's description of the skills necessary for success in the dean of students' role have stayed constant over the years. The book articulated that a dean needed

> high energy levels; ability to initiate; effective coping with daily pressures, uncertainty and ambiguities; high regard for competence and integrity in themselves and for their staffs; sensitivity to the needs of those around them; a recognition or awareness of the personal and institutional values that guide behavior; good relationships with students, staff, faculty and colleagues. (p. 1)

In fact, the book's description of these dean of students' success skills really apply to any who hold a senior role in student affairs. This begs the following question: What is unique and necessary about the dean of students' position on a college campus?

Answering the preceding question is difficult, because there is no universal definition of a *dean of students*. Munin describes in chapter 1 that most laypersons' belief is based on popular portrayal of the dean in movies, that the dean has some responsibility for student discipline. And a quotation from Jim Rhatigan (former VPSA, Wichita State University, and contributing author in this book) that "the role of the Dean historically included the assignment of the disciplinary responsibility to the dean's office" reinforces this notion of the dean as disciplinarian (Appleton, 1978, p. 103). Munin's chapter also describes the historical development and evolution of the position from the first deans of men and women to the variety of ways in which the dean of students' position exists at today's colleges and universities. At some institutions the dean of students is the most senior student affairs officer and responsible for oversight of the entire student affairs operation on the campus. At other institutions the dean of students is one of a number of staff reporting to a VPSA, has a portfolio of units reporting to him or her, and is often seen as the second in command to the VPSA.

To gather some more information, I posted a question to a VPSA electronic mailing list. I asked my colleagues to define the dean of students' role from their perspective and, as the practice of student affairs continues to evolve, whether the dean of students' position (in addition to the VPSA) should continue to exist. Here are a few responses:

> We have trained the outside world (parents and students specifically) that the [deans of students] title has meaning and significance—it is where you go when you need help, support, or assistance.

> Many of our positions (i.e., vice presidents for student affairs) have become more executive, demonstrating the need for both the VPSA and the [dean of students].

> I think we are struggling to hold onto the dean of students' role for more romantic and historical reasons than because the role has unique and contemporary responsibilities. When we ascribe to a dean of students a sense that he/she is expected to be the chief student advocate/crisis officer or the like, we denigrate and diminish the role of the senior student affairs officer.

> I still take the position that the title is outdated and unnecessary. Responses from colleagues about the various ways in which the dean of students' position is organized on their campus demonstrate there is no common role for those who hold the title; each has a distinctive portfolio. Many divisions of student affairs have multiple associate/assistant VPSA roles, and it is easier for folks to understand that the VPSA oversees the entire operation of the division, and associate/assistant VPSAs oversee assorted components assigned to them.

> We have overburdened the role of the [dean of students] with too much supervisory authority and co-titling them as AVCs and [deans of students]. A previous supervisor would routinely say the [dean of students] was her number two and the moral compass of the university.

> I think one challenge is that too often crisis management work defines our VPSA roles in the eyes of others, and it can be hard as a VP to let the dean of students flourish in that role. And, if an AVP/[dean of students] position is created, the AVP/[dean of students] may see their portfolio as more important than that of the other AVPs. I created a [dean of

students] role when I got to my current institution, as the existing dean of students only had a conduct portfolio, which I believe shortchanged the role in terms of positive relationships with students, community building, and having their pulse on the campus climate.

I have a number of associate VPSAs, and one of those is the AVP and dean of students. This person has departments under them, but the title of dean of students puts them in the public as the first line if the students are having issues. Students get to the [dean of students] before they get to me (the VPSA). Could I do without the title—yes. I will tell you that those in the position cherish the title because it is advantageous on their CV and for promotional purposes.

When I (the VPSA) meet with people—students, alumni, parents—I am often described by them as the dean of students—hardly anyone in public knows me as the VPSA (or knows what a VPSA is or does).

Sometimes there is a danger that an AVP/[dean of students] may see their portfolio as more important than that of the other AVPs.

I have never had a [dean of students]. I believe this role in the future will be entirely based on the composition and context of each individual school. Regardless, the basis and important functions of overseeing student activities and student activism will always exist. Every other function a [dean of students] might or might not assume supervisory leadership for in the future (judicial, spiritual life, health, and residence life) can be assumed by another AVP or other staff.

I continue to be asked the difference between my role as VPSA and the dean of students; I am struggling a bit to explain it to others since I just know it when I see it.

I hold both titles (VPSA and [dean of students]) and that works at my institution.

So what are we to take away from the preceding noncongruent perspectives on the dean of students' position and in particular the question as to whether there is still a need for a dean of students? It seems, based on the responses from my colleagues, that the answer to the need for the dean of students' position by title is not universally "yes." However, I would argue, based on the preceding chapters in this book and the answers of some of my colleagues, there exists core roles and responsibilities, often ascribed to the dean, that are important for institutions of higher education. I also believe that the title *dean* connotes something familiar and important to internal and external audiences and is a traditional academic title that may still have important meaning on a college campus. Finally, as a VPSA myself, I know firsthand the importance of having a strong leadership team and to have a person or persons on my leadership team whom the rest of the campus knows to call when I am away.

Therefore, even though my VPSA colleagues have varied responses to whether having a dean of students is still necessary in student affairs, on the basis of the preceding chapters in this book, I think there are some areas of agreement.

There are some critical student affairs leadership responsibilities for all who hold senior student affairs leadership positions. There exist some core areas of emphasis that are an important part of student affairs work, particularly at the leadership level. This book highlights some vital responsibilities, often ascribed to the dean of students' position, that include, among other things, the ability to respond to any number of student crises; serve as a student advocate; be knowledge-able about a range of local, state, and federal policies; be a mentor to students and to staff; supervise a range of student affairs departments and areas; interact regularly with the president or chancellor, board of trustee members, community members, parents, and alumni; and engage in complex problem-solving. I believe my colleagues and I would agree that the aforementioned, along with many others, are indeed important aspects of senior student affairs leadership work. I think my colleagues and I also do not believe that it is *only* someone who holds a dean of students' title who must be knowledgeable and engage in this important work—all of us who work in student affairs at the senior leadership level must have this knowledge and ability.

A vice president for student affairs needs a strong leadership team, which does not have to include a dean of students, though it may. VPSAs are generally charged with the overall responsibility for leading and managing an array of student affairs functions and for leading the overall strategic vision for student affairs work on our campuses. For those of us in the VPSA role to do our jobs well, having a strong leadership team is critical, as we alone do not have the capacity to manage the day-to-day activities of each area in our division while also serving as executive leaders of the institution as a whole. The functional areas overseen by the members of our respective student affairs leadership teams are reflective of the organizational needs and strategic focus of our institutions, so the portfolios of the members of our leadership teams vary. In addition, some of us have organizational charts with several associate and assistant vice presidents with relatively equal status, and others of us may have a clear number two in our organization. For those of us who have someone, other than ourselves, with the title of dean of students in our organization, that person is most typically designated as the number-two person in our division and often, as described by more than one of my colleagues, the senior student affairs leader who is most student facing. This student-facing role is particularly important given the broad executive leadership role that the VPSA is charged with on campus.

A dean of students by role and title could be an important one depending on the institutional context. It is interesting to read the responses from my VPSA colleagues about whether the dean of students, role and title, is still important. Some argue that we are clinging to the role and title because of history and tradition and that the title and role are less meaningful because there is no standard job description across the student affairs discipline for a dean of students. Others say that the role and title connote something important on their campus, whether because the dean of students is seen as the primary student advocate on campus or has a particularly campus-important set of responsibilities to coordinate and oversee. Sometimes it is the case that the dean of students is the only title students, parents, and others at the university really understand relative to student affairs work. After all, many do not really know what a VPSA is or does. (As I write this, my institution just completed parents' weekend. When I was introduced over and over as the dean of students by parents and some of my colleagues outside of student affairs, I chuckled remembering that at least one of my colleagues surveyed said she has the same experience on her campus. In other words, no one has any clue what the title of vice chancellor for student affairs means—but they are familiar enough with the title of dean of students and figure that must be what I am!) Another point of view is that the title *dean* is a traditional academic title, and at some institutions assigning the dean title in student affairs helps underscore the connection between student affairs and academic affairs. Although I would also add that we diminish the power of using the title of dean in student affairs as a link to the academic side of the house when the person holding the dean title in student affairs does not have anything related to academics or academic partnerships in their portfolio. In addition, for many in our profession, the dean of students' position is seen as the next step in the ladder toward becoming a VPSA. While the point has been made throughout this book about the varied portfolios overseen by those who hold a dean of students' title, the dean of students' title can be an important next-step symbol for those who desire to become VPSAs and those who are recruiting for VPSA positions.

In summary, at least on the basis of my small survey of my colleagues, we do not have universal agreement about whether the title and role are still important or consistent across campuses—the answer appears to be "it depends." The challenge, however, with "it depends" is that it can be difficult to articulate to the campus president and other leaders the need for a dean of students separate and distinct from the VPSA. As a profession, if we could more clearly articulate core functions for a dean of students' position within the student affairs discipline, that might strengthen a VPSA's ability to advocate for the dean of students position. So, in the following section, I offer some thoughts for what I believe to be the essence of a dean of students' position.

The Dean of Students Should Be . . .

The dean of students should be student facing. A dean of students should be the most senior student-facing position in student affairs such that students (and parents and others) know that if there is a critical student issue or concern that needs attention, the dean of students is the person in student affairs charged with responding. Like so many student affairs professionals, I decided on a career in student affairs because I had an interest in working with students. My early days in the field were spent in many positions that directly advised students and student organizations. As I moved up the administrative ladder to the vice chancellor for student affairs position, I now spend much of my time managing people, policies, and processes and sadly a lot less time each day working with students. Certainly, those in my position must continue to find ways to have frequent contact with students, and VPSAs play a critical role in shaping the overall quality of the student experience on campus. However, VPSAs are not also always readily available to immediately respond to student issues (though VPSAs will always be on the front lines for significant campus crises), and it is important that the VPSA has a member of the team whose formal role is to be that touch point for students regarding everyday student concerns. By title alone, the dean of students is perhaps most commonly understood to be the face of the administration for students.

The dean of students should be more than the campus disciplinarian. Much has been made of the view of the dean of students as campus disciplinarian, and I suspect if a survey was conducted of deans of students' portfolios across colleges and universities, almost all would have some responsibility for student conduct. While some kind of office for student conduct and community standards seems to be a standard student affairs department reporting up to the dean of students, our emeriti VPSAs and at least one of my VPSA colleagues who participated in the electronic mailing list conversation believe that at its core, the role of the dean of students is much broader than chief disciplinarian and is to serve as the *moral compass* for the campus. What does it mean to serve as the moral compass for the campus? In the early formation of colleges and universities, faculty saw the moral and character development of students as a critical aspect of a college education and of their responsibilities as faculty members. However, a recent article in *The Chronicle of*

Higher Education titled *"How Professors Ceded Their Authority"* (Wellmon, 2018) offered commentary on faculty abdicating this particular role to student affairs professionals.

> Within almost all colleges and universities, with the exception of some religiously affiliated institutions (and even then unevenly), moral education has shifted from the curriculum—from classrooms and labs—to extracurricular student life. (p. 5)
>
> When universities shifted moral education out of their curricula and into the realm of extracurriculars, they relieved faculty members of responsibility for the ethical formation of their students. And the faculty members consented, grateful for the time to focus on other administrative operations or their research. Professional administrative staff members gradually took on the responsibility for character and moral education. (p. 7)

In other words, this article argued that to the extent colleges are focused on the moral and ethical formation of students, that education takes place largely outside of the classroom, in areas that are more typically in the realm of student affairs. The aforementioned reinforces the notion of moving our thinking of the dean of students beyond chief disciplinarian to the idea of the dean as the moral compass for the campus. In so doing that means the core work of the dean of students should be to facilitate the ethical and character development of students and to role model and reinforce the institutional values of our campuses through our interactions with students and as a part of the decision-making on issues that affect student life (e.g., if our institution states that it values diversity, how do we ensure that value shows up in our institutional strategic planning, our response to student issues, and our day-to-day work?).

The dean of students should be assigned the most critical strategic student affairs functions in their portfolio. In the electronic mailing list conversations with my colleagues about defining the dean of students' role, some comments focused on the idea that the lack of a common set of dean of students' responsibilities across institutions made it difficult to advocate for the creation of a dean of students' position on a campus where this role had not historically existed (or was not separate from the VPSA position) and/or articulate the unique value of the dean of students' role on a campus. Certainly, there is often value in the student affairs profession in benchmarking positions across our institutions (we often use benchmarking to convince our presidents or chancellors, provosts, boards of trustee, and so on that we need a particular position, program, or salary level to maintain our competitive advantage against other institutions to whom we compare ourselves). However, I am intrigued by a few of my VPSA colleagues who, instead of organizing the portfolios for their dean of students' positions primarily around the more typical responsibilities for student conduct and crisis management, conceptualized the dean of students as the person focused on the most critical strategic needs for the division and campus. For example, Ryan Lombardi created the first dean of students' position at Cornell University centered on equity, access, and social justice—critical issues on most of our campuses though not the typically principal functions of the dean of students on most campuses. As a new VPSA to Cornell, Lombardi identified a number of challenges around issues of diversity and inclusion in the Cornell student community and wanted to emphasize, by creating a dean of students' job description with equity, access, and social justice at the center, that the Division of Student and Campus Life at Cornell would make these issues paramount to the work of the division and the university. On campuses where student retention is a critical strategic issue, some of my colleagues have assigned retention-related functions to the dean of students' portfolio—for example, orientation and transition programs, advising and mentoring programs, and centers for first-generation and low-income students. And I have seen others reconceptualize the dean of students' position as the chief wellness officer for the campus with oversight for health and wellness functions. Given the unique challenges of our respective campuses, rather than thinking we strengthen our advocacy for the importance of the dean of students' position by working toward a common set of responsibilities for deans of students across the student affairs profession, I think each VPSA needs to articulate the value of having a dean of students who, given the breadth of VPSA responsibilities, can focus in a concentrated way on the most critical student and student life needs toward helping the institution achieve its overall mission.

The dean of students should be considered a member of the Institutional Council of Academic Deans. It seems that we continue to spend a lot of time in student affairs discussing (and sometimes kvetching about) our relationship with our academic colleagues (often in the vein of how we can get our academic colleagues to understand and respect student affairs). I would hope that by this juncture in the field of student affairs (with NASPA–Student Affairs Administrators in Higher Education and American College Personnel Association [ACPA] each being over 95 years old at the time of this publication and with a firm theoretical and research base for our work as student affairs professionals), we would have long moved past these conversations and consternations about the place of student affairs in the academy. That said, there are still wonderful opportunities to connect with our academic colleagues toward working collectively to achieve our respective institutional missions. Earlier in this piece I contended that we diminish the power of using the title *dean*, a historically academic title, in student affairs if the person holding the title of dean does not have anything related to academics or academic partnerships in their portfolio. For the dean of students to be viewed on par with academic deans in terms of stature and influence, that means positioning the work of the dean of students toward intentional support of the educational and academic mission of the institution.

The dean of students should be a pipeline to the VPSA position. While not all deans of students will want to become VPSAs, many will. Those of us who supervise the dean of students should ensure that we are providing our deans of students with the experiences they will need to compete successfully for a VPSA position should they choose to pursue one. In addition to those must-have experiences that VPSA search committees are most often looking for in prospective candidates (e.g., experiences overseeing budgets, supervising staff, leading initiatives, managing crises, to name a few), it is also important we provide opportunities for our dean of students to interact with boards of trustees, be exposed to institutional-level planning and decision-making, and become involved in complex problem-solving. An effective VPSA is one who is engaged at a strategic level and can communicate effectively with other senior university leaders, governing boards, and various stakeholders. If there are particular skill areas where we think our dean of students needs additional training, we should be committed to providing him or her with professional development opportunities either on campus or through the multitude of programs offered through various professional associations. NASPA and ACPA both have outstanding aspiring VPSA institutes. For women in leadership specifically, NASPA offers the Alice Manicur Symposium, and Bryn Mawr has a program called HERS. The Harvard Institutes for Higher Education also has several excellent summer institutes focused on higher education leadership.

In addition, we must be committed to expanding the dean of students pipeline and making sure we encourage and groom mid-level professionals from a variety of student affairs disciplines to consider the role of dean of students. Often, in filling the role of dean of students, we look to those who have previously served as directors of student conduct or worked in residential life or fraternity and sorority life (all are certainly great launching points for positions as deans of students, particularly those more traditional dean of students' roles), and we overlook our colleagues who are working in the multicultural and LGBTQ centers or other areas of student affairs and/or the university that are not always thought of as the pathway to the position of dean of students. I had one of those nontraditional pathways to the dean of students and VPSA positions. I started my career in student affairs as the director of the cross-cultural center at the University of California, Irvine. While I later spent a few years working in residential life and student activities, my formation as a student affairs professional occurred during the six years I spent working in multicultural student affairs. It was there I learned the positive impact of dedicated spaces for students of color on marginalized students' sense of belonging at a predominantly White institution; the importance of creating inclusive communities to enhance the learning environment for all students (inclusive learning communities are vital for all students, not just students of color); to be an effective advocate for the voices of students who felt they had long been unheard at the university; and navigated the challenges of working with diverse groups of students with different perspectives to create a shared welcoming space for all students who used the center. These are experiences and skills I call on every day in my work as a VPSA. I later moved to the dean of students' position from serving as an assistant vice provost for undergraduate education— a position in academic affairs overseeing academic advising and a student learning center. It took a VPSA with an open mind about who might be best suited for the new dean of students' position he created to see that my background working in academic affairs would be an asset in forging a closer connection on his campus between student affairs, the provost's office, and the academic schools. I am not sure I would have made it through the search committee process otherwise.

So What Is a Dean of Students . . . Really?

When my coeditor Art Munin and I sat down to think about the framework for this book, we wanted to make sure we had perspectives from someone who was newly in the position, someone who was seasoned, and someone who had retired from the position and could provide a retrospective. For the retrospective we were fortunate to persuade James J. Rhatigan and James W. Lyons, two pillars of the profession, to contribute a chapter to this book. Reading their chapter should remind us all of the core focus, from their perspective, of a dean of students—to be teacher, educator, student advocate, role model, and moral compass for the institution. Those of us who have been fortunate to have been mentored by one or both of these two incredible men will remember they taught us that being a dean of students is to remember the importance of making personal connections with students and colleagues, to not be afraid to raise critical questions and challenge other institutional leaders when we think those leaders are drifting away from core institutional mission and values, to speak up and speak out about important issues affecting students and our communities, and to think about how we would respond to an issue or a problem not because the law compels us to act but because we know what is the right thing to do. In fact, as an aside, even when Lyons was offered the title of VPSA at Stanford, he refused to accept the title because he felt the title of vice president moved him away from what he believed to be the core focus and ideals of *deaning*.

Given there has not been a book written about deans of students since 1978, for those who are a dean of students or are seeking to become or appoint one at this particular moment in time (circa early twenty-first century), this book provides a great overview of the varied work of the dean of students, the challenges and rewards of the work, the skills a dean of students should have, and the information a dean of students should know to be successful in the position.

I will leave you with what I think is a fitting way to end this book, which is with a quote from *Pieces of Eight* (Appleton, 1978), a book about deans of students. When asked what a dean is, one of the contributors to that book said, "I had no clear authority and probably no obligation, but my own sense of what was right led me to move anyway" (p. 66).

References

Appleton, J. (1978). *Pieces of eight: The rites, roles, and styles of the dean, by eight who have been there*. Washington, DC: NASPA. Retrieved from https://files.eric.ed.gov/fulltext/ED292432.pdf

Wellmon, C. (2018, November 20). How professors ceded their authority: Education and moral purpose have parted ways. *The Chronicle of Higher Education*. Retrieved from https://www.chronicle.com/article/How-Professors-Ceded-Their/245133

EDITORS AND CONTRIBUTORS

Editors

Art Munin serves as associate vice chancellor and dean of students at the University of Wisconsin, Oshkosh. Previously, Munin held leadership positions at Illinois State University, DePaul University, the School of the Art Institute, and Loyola University Chicago. In addition to his varying administrative roles, Munin has served as an instructional assistant professor in the College Student Personnel Administration at Illinois State University and as an adjunct professor in Loyola University Chicago's higher education program. As a writer, he has coauthored chapters in the books *Closing the Opportunity Gap: Identity-Conscious Strategies for Retention and Student Success* (Stylus, 2016) and *Handbook for Student Leadership Development* (Jossey-Bass, 2011). He authored *Color by Number: Understanding Racism Through Facts and Stats on Children* (Stylus, 2012) and coauthored *The Diversity Consultant Cookbook: Preparing for the Challenge* (Stylus, 2019). As a complement to this work, Munin has served in several capacities through NASPA–Student Affairs Administrators in Higher Education, including the chair of the AVP Steering Committee, AVP Institute codirector and faculty, the associate editor for the *Journal of Student Affairs Research and Practice*, and a member of the Civic Learning and Democratic Engagement Initiative and the regional conference planning committee. Finally, Munin has served as a diversity educator and consultant for institutions across the United States for 15 years through his company Art Munin Consulting (artmunin.com).

Munin earned a PhD in higher education and an MEd in community counseling at Loyola University Chicago, an MA in multicultural communication at DePaul University, and a BA in psychology from Eastern Illinois University. Outside of higher education, Munin has played guitar for 25 years and loves to share music with his twin 7-year-olds (Ava and Vincent) and his wife Heidi.

Lori S. White is the vice chancellor for students at Washington University in St. Louis. White has spent over 30 years working in higher education. Prior to her arrival at Washington University, she served as the vice president for student affairs and clinical professor of education at Southern Methodist University. She also worked at the University of Southern California, Stanford; Georgetown University; San Diego State University; and the University of California, Irvine. At Washington University, White and her colleagues are responsible for a range of student life programs including residence halls, student activities, student leadership programs, student conduct, the Center for Diversity and Inclusion, the First Year Center, health and wellness programs, career services, student academic support programs, international students and scholars, scholarship programs, the Danforth University Center, and Washington University athletics and recreational programs.

White is active nationally in several higher education organizations and has served on the board of directors for the Association for Sustainability in Higher Education (AASHE) and NASPA. In 2009, she was named a Pillar of the Profession by NASPA. White was elected chair of the NASPA board of directors for 2016–2017.

White's areas of emphasis in research and teaching include the student experience in higher education and the preparation and mentorship of new, mid-level, and aspiring senior student affairs professionals. She is the author of a number of articles and book chapters and has presented widely at professional meetings. Her most recent publication is a coedited volume titled *Transformational Encounters: Shaping Diverse College and University Leaders* (NASPA, 2018).

White was born and raised in San Francisco, California. She earned a BA in psychology and English from the University of California, Berkeley, and a PhD in education administration and policy analysis with emphasis in higher education from Stanford University. She also participated in Harvard University's Management and Leadership in Education Program. Her claim to fame is that she can name the mascot of just about every Division I college (and she is working on learning all of the mascots for Division III).

Contributors

Akirah J. Bradley is the associate vice chancellor for student affairs for the University of Colorado, Boulder (CU Boulder). Bradley's previous position at CU Boulder was the dean of students and associate vice chancellor for student affairs. In addition to working for CU Boulder, she has served in various leadership positions at the University of California, Berkeley, and on Semester at Sea. Highlights of her experience include auxiliary services, housing and dining, student development, student conduct, student union, behavioral intervention teams, residence life, and crisis response. Bradley is recognized as an administrator who leads with integrity, equity, compassion, and student advocacy at the center. She earned her EdD in educational leadership from the University of California, Davis. Her research focus is qualitative exploration of administrators' response to university crises and support systems available to assist administrators in the aftermath of crisis. She also has her MEd in higher education student affairs administration from the University of Vermont and a BS in business administration from Mansfield University in Pennsylvania. Bradley has presented at national and regional conferences, taught university courses, and published articles in higher education journals.

Jacob Diaz serves as the regional assistant vice chancellor for student affairs and dean of students at the University of South Florida, Saint Petersburg, where he oversees a diverse portfolio of areas. In this capacity, he also serves as the deputy Title IX coordinator. His purpose in the profession is to create an environment where all students can cultivate their dreams. Professionally, Diaz has had a gifted career. He had the privilege of serving as vice president for student development at Seattle University, where he provided strategic leadership for a comprehensive portfolio of student services and programs. He has also held professional roles in student affairs such as assistant vice president and dean of students, Seattle University; assistant dean for conduct, policy, and climate, University of Vermont; director, Center for Student Ethics and Standards, University of Vermont; and special assistant to the dean of students, University of Vermont. In addition to his administrative posts, he has had the privilege of serving as a faculty member teaching graduate and undergraduate courses in leadership and governance of higher education, community engagement, and leadership. Diaz's BA is from the University of California, Santa Barbara, and both his MA and PhD are from the University of Vermont. He was a Bill and Melinda Gates Foundation Millennium Scholar and participated in Harvard's Management and Leadership in Education program.

Anne Flaherty has led in student affairs for over 20 years. She currently serves as interim associate vice chancellor for student support and wellness at Washington University in St. Louis, where she leads the wellness cluster including the Habif Health and Wellness Center, RSVP (Relationship and Sexual Violence Prevention Center), and the WashU Cares behavior intervention team. Prior to this role, she served as both the dean of student life and the interim vice president for student affairs at Butler University. She has also led at two different medical centers as the assistant dean for medical student affairs at Indiana University School of Medicine and at the University of Kansas Medical Center as assistant dean of students and registrar. Her first professional role was at Park University in Kansas City as the director of residence life. Flaherty earned her bachelor's degree in psychology at the University of Iowa, a master's in higher education administration from the University of Kansas, and a doctoral degree in higher education administration with a minor in health policy and management also from the University of Kansas. Flaherty has been an active member of NASPA throughout her career. She currently serves as a member of NASPA's AVP Steering Committee and is a part of the 2017–2019 NASPA SERVE (Supporting, Expanding, and Recruiting Volunteer Excellence) Academy cohort. Highlights of her NASPA involvement are serving as a cochair for the NASPA IV-West conference in Breckenridge, Colorado, in 2006 and starting the NASPA Undergraduate Fellows Program at the University of Kansas.

Adam Goldstein serves as the associate vice president for campus life and dean of students at Wake Forest University. In this role, he supports a family of student-centered, community-facing offices, including Student Conduct, Student Engagement, Student Organization Finance and Operations, CARE Team and Case Management Services, Intercultural Center, Pro Humanitate Institute, and Orientation. Before joining the Wake Forest community, Goldstein served as associate dean of students at Florida State University, assistant dean for campus life and director of campus activities at Drexel University, and director of student activities at Georgia Southwestern State University. His professional activities include five years of service as faculty for hazingprevention.org's Novak Institute for Hazing Prevention and four years of service as faculty for the Association of Student Conduct Administration's (ASCA) Gehring Academy. In 2013, Goldstein received ASCA's Award of Excellence for his work supporting the development of new professionals and advancing knowledge about learning-centered practice and assessment in student conduct settings. Goldstein holds a BA in English from Indiana University of Pennsylvania (1992) and an MA (1994) and a PhD (2004) in student affairs administration from the University of Georgia.

Anna Gonzalez serves as vice president for student affairs and dean of students at Harvey Mudd College, a member of the Claremont Colleges in Southern California. With over 25 years of professional experience in higher education, Gonzalez served as the dean and chief student affairs officer at Lewis and Clark College; the associate vice chancellor at the University of Illinois at Urbana–Champaign; and the associate dean of students at the University of California, Irvine, and she sailed four times as the dean of students with Semester at Sea. She is also the founding member, and continues to teach in the Student Affairs Program at Lewis and Clark College's graduate school. Gonzalez is the coeditor of the 2018 NASPA publication titled *Transformational Encounters: Shaping Diverse College and University Leaders* and has received numerous awards, including NASPA's Pillar of the Profession and the Scott Goodnight Award for Outstanding Dean. Through partnerships with on- and off-campus stakeholders, Gonzalez is guided by the vision of advancing the educational mission of higher education, creating an accessible educational experience for all individuals, and helping students become global leaders of the twenty-first century.

Bridget Turner Kelly is associate professor of student affairs at the University of Maryland. She received her MA and PhD in social foundations of education from the University of Maryland. For the past 9 years, she was associate professor and program chair of higher education at Loyola University Chicago. Prior to that, Kelly was associate professor of student development at Seattle University and assistant professor of higher education and student affairs at the University of Vermont. Her scholarship focuses on marginalized populations in higher education, such as Women and Faculty of Color. She has authored over 25 publications, including 2 articles that have received over 200 citations each and 2 that have been cited in AMICUS briefs for U.S. Supreme Court cases. Kelly is an award-winning teacher of intergroup dialogue and presents nationally on the topic. She is an author in and coeditor of *Engaging Images for Research, Pedagogy, and Practice: Utilizing Visuals to Understand and Promote College Student Development* (Stylus, 2017). Kelly met her partner, Robert D. Kelly, while they were both graduate students at the University of Maryland, and they have been married for over 16 years.

Robert D. Kelly is the university vice president and special assistant to the president at Loyola University Maryland. Deeply immersed in both liberal arts and Jesuit education, he provides leadership, counsel, and coordination of initiatives across the institution in support of the strategic plan and institutional objectives. Prior to his position, he served in executive roles as chief of staff at Union College, New York, and vice president for student development both at Loyola University Chicago and at Seattle University. He has also served in various administrative and research roles at the University of Maryland and the University of Vermont. He began his professional career at Colgate University, New York. In addition to his administrative positions, Kelly has been a clinical professor, teaching a number of courses at both graduate and undergraduate levels, and has published and presented papers on various aspects of leadership and college life. Kelly received a BA in political science from Loyola University Maryland. He holds an MA in higher education administration from the University of Vermont and a PhD in higher education from the University of Maryland.

James W. Lyons completed his undergraduate liberal arts studies at Allegheny College. His major studies were economics, and his minors were philosophy and history. He worked his way through with part-time jobs, including a year as student assistant to the dean of students and as a residence assistant. He earned his graduate degrees at Indiana University and initially enrolled in the School of Business where he studied management and business law. Then he transferred to the School of Education when he discovered courses that would fuel a career in student affairs. Lyons served as a resident adviser but was soon appointed program coordinator of the Indiana Memorial Union and then as assistant director. Robert Shaffer became his most influential mentor and chaired his graduate committee. At the end of his degree program, he was asked by Haverford College to be its first dean of students. He served in that post for 10 years. When Lyons was asked to join Stanford, he was offered the titles of "vice president" or "dean" of student affairs. He chose the latter, because "dean" connoted an educational role. He served as dean for 18 years. Along the way, he was appointed as a lecturer in the Graduate School of Education. When he retired as dean, he directed a graduate program in higher education for 7 years. Lyons was active in NASPA and a regular presenter at regional and national meetings, and he organized weeklong workshops for deans and college presidents. He was the 1988 recipient of NASPA's Scott Goodnight Award. He served as a consultant or an accreditor for more than 45 colleges and universities across the nation. When he retired, Stanford created the James W. Lyons Award for Service that is presented annually to 8 graduate and undergraduate students. All who knew him were saddened with the news that James W. Lyons passed away on February 9, 2019. He will be greatly missed.

Marla Morgen serves as the associate vice president of legal and governmental affairs at the Higher Learning Commission (HLC). Prior to joining HLC, Morgen spent over a decade in the Office of the General Counsel at DePaul University. As senior associate general counsel, Morgen provided advice and legal counsel on a wide range of issues such as student conduct, sexual and relationship violence and Title IX, speech and expression issues, campus safety, student activities, housing, disability issues, student welfare and mental health, academic integrity, international programs, admissions, employment, diversity, public relations, and experiential education. Morgen is a frequent presenter on issues such as student conduct, sexual violence and Title IX, servicing students with disabilities, and experiential education, particularly internships. Morgen received her JD from the University of Michigan and received her BA in American history from Northwestern University.

Vijay Pendakur serves as the Robert W. and Elizabeth C. Staley dean of students at Cornell University. Prior to this appointment, he worked on campus-wide student success initiatives for underserved populations as an associate vice president for student affairs at California State University, Fullerton. Before joining the team at Fullerton, Pendakur served as the director for the Office of Multicultural Student Success at DePaul University in Chicago. He is the editor of the recent book *Closing the Opportunity Gap: Identity-Conscious Strategies for Retention and Student Success* (Stylus, 2016) and numerous chapters on racial identity development, critical leadership pedagogy, and student affairs administration. Pendakur serves on the institute teaching faculty of the Center for Race and Equity at the University of Southern California and as a faculty member for the Institute on High-Impact Practices and Student Success through the Association of American Colleges and Universities. He currently serves on the National Institutes of Health (NIH) Working Group on Diversity, which advises the director of the NIH on inclusion and equity strategy in the field of biomedical research. He holds a BA in history and East Asian studies from the University of Wisconsin, Madison; an MA in U.S. history from the University of California, San Diego; and a PhD in education from DePaul University.

James J. Rhatigan spent the preponderance of his long career at Wichita State University as vice president for student affairs and dean of students beginning in 1965, following 5 years as an assistant dean of men at the University of Iowa. His reputation was built by promoting student success and protecting students' rights as citizens. He served as the president of NASPA in 1975 and was the NASPA historian from 1976 to 1997. He is a frequent contributor to the literature, writing numerous articles and book chapters. He also has written, coauthored, or edited 4 books and monographs. Rhatigan was on the board of The Freshman Year experience for 25 years and a consultant and evaluator for the Higher Learning Commission for more than 20 years. He received the Fred Turner Award (for service to NASPA) in 1980 and the Scott Goodnight Award (for outstanding performance as a dean) in 1987. His BA degree is from Coe College, and his MA degree is from Syracuse University, both in American history, and he earned a PhD from the University of Iowa in student personnel administration. The student center at Wichita State was named in his honor in 1996. He is the cofounder of the WSU Regional Institute on Aging and raised the money to endow it.

Lauren Scott Rivera serves as the assistant vice president for student life and dean of students at the University of Scranton. In this role, she works tirelessly as the lead student advocate while overseeing the following departments in fostering transformative learning experiences: Center for Health Education and Wellness, Center for Student Engagement, Cross Cultural Centers (Jane Kopas Women's Center and Multicultural Center), and residence life. She also serves as deputy Title IX coordinator for students and advises student government. In 2009, Rivera began her work in Catholic and Jesuit higher education at the University of Scranton as the director of student conduct and assessment. Prior to joining the Scranton community, she worked at the Pennsylvania State University in the Office of Judicial Affairs. Rivera holds a BA in political science and religion from Bucknell University. She developed a joint degree program at the Pennsylvania State University through which she earned her MA in college student affairs and her JD from the Pennsylvania State University's Dickinson School of Law.

Penny Rue serves as vice president for campus life at Wake Forest University, with broad responsibility for the safety and well-being of students and their education outside the classroom. Rue previously served as vice chancellor for student affairs at the University of California, San Diego. She has over 40 years of experience, including leadership roles at the University of Virginia and Georgetown University. Early in her career she worked at the University of Maryland and the University of North Carolina at Chapel Hill. She is known for her creative leadership in strengthening campus communities. Rue received her doctorate in counseling and personnel services from the University of Maryland, where her research focused on a conceptual study of community on the college campus. She has an MA in student personnel services from The Ohio State University and a BA in English and religion *magna cum laude* from Duke University. She was honored as a NASPA Pillar of the Profession and as a recipient of the Maude Stewart Distinguished Alumna Award from The Ohio State University in 2011. She currently serves as chair of the board of directors for NASPA.

Shadia Sachedina embraces the opportunity to make a positive difference in the lives of people. Her experience as a student affairs educator spans over 25 years, and she approaches her work with a firm commitment and passion for working with people to help them uncover their true potential. Sachedina currently serves as the assistant vice president for student success and the dean of students at the Fashion Institute of Technology with the State University of New York. She has worked in a variety of functional areas within student affairs, including residence life, student activities, leadership development, student conduct, and orientation and first-year experience programs at different institutions. Sachedina has taught graduate courses in leadership in higher education and student affairs in higher education, as well as a seminar in critical decision-making in student affairs practice. A Gallup-certified strengths coach, Sachedina works with students and colleagues to help them uncover their true talent potential so that they can become stronger leaders and better managers. She is currently working on a graduate certification in restorative practices at the International Institute of Restorative Practices. Most recently, Sachedina serves as a faculty member for the 2019 NASPA AVP Institute. She has a BA in English from Stony Brook University, SUNY; an MS in higher education administration from Baruch College, CUNY; and an EdD in higher education administration from New York University.

Denise Balfour Simpson serves as the director of academic initiatives at Duke Kunshan University, located in the Jiangsu province of China, and holds an adjunct faculty position at the University of North Carolina at Charlotte. Prior to these roles, she served as the dean of students and chief student affairs officer at Johnson and Wales University, Charlotte Campus, and has additional experiences in student conduct, residence life, campus recreation, and student involvement. Simpson's passion for student affairs lies with alternative dispute resolution and restorative justice practices and the development of new student affairs professionals. She has several publications related to supporting student conduct programs and high-impact practices surrounding student engagement. When not engaged in campus life, she finds solace in traveling with her partner; teaching group fitness classes; and spending quality time with her cockapoo, Anakin. Simpson holds a PhD in higher education from Old Dominion University; an MEd in educational leadership from the University of Nevada, Las Vegas; and a BA in psychology and communication studies from DePaul University.

Sue Wasiolek, for the past 40 years (except for a brief 9-month hiatus to practice law), has worked in the Division of Student Affairs at Duke University. During this time, she has served as the assistant to the dean for student life and the dean for student life, and she currently works as an associate vice president for student affairs and dean of students. Her areas of responsibility and oversight have included new student orientation, judicial affairs, residential life, parent programs, fraternity and sorority life, disability services, leadership development, case management, student health and wellness, counseling and psychological services, mediation, crisis response, and numerous "other duties as assigned." She has served for over 35 years as an academic adviser to freshmen and sophomores and has taught courses in education, law, and cultural anthropology. She has a BA in science education, an MHA, and an ML from Duke University. She has also completed a JD from North Carolina Central University and an EdD from the University of Pennsylvania. Having served as a peer reviewer for the NCAA, Wasiolek enjoys intercollegiate athletics from an intellectual and spectator perspective. Her master's of law thesis was titled "Intercollegiate Athletics and Federal Income Tax Policy," and her doctoral dissertation focused on the efficacy of the NCAA self-study certification process. In 2008, she coauthored a book titled *Getting the Best Out of College* (Ten Speed Press), with the second edition released in March 2012. She currently resides in an all-freshman residence hall at Duke and loves it!

Rob Wild is an associate vice chancellor for student affairs and dean of students at Washington University in St. Louis. In this role he oversees the Office of Residential Life, the Office of Student Conduct and Community Standards, Campus Life (which includes student government and fraternity and sorority life), and the First Year Center. An important goal of these departments is to ensure the successful transition of students into the university. These areas bring a focus for all students on student development, leadership, and engagement. Wild has significant previous experience in student affairs at both Washington University and the University of Wisconsin, and prior to his current role, he served as the assistant and chief of staff to Chancellor Mark S. Wrighton. Wild has over 10 years of professional experience in residential life. He holds a bachelor of arts degree in biology and African and African American studies from Washington University, a master of science degree in educational administration from the University of Wisconsin, and a doctorate in education from the University of Missouri, St. Louis.

as student affairs professionals goal, 3
student body and senior campus
    leadership connection of, 56, 73
student learning and success issues
    of, 28
success experiencing of, 4
supervision scope of, 3
support needs of, 9
topics covered about, 9
work and family balance question
    to, 79
dean of students, colleagues advice for,
    4, 169
as adviser and mentor and friend,
    111, 112
approachability quality for, 110–11
big picture seeing ability of, 105
campus community visibility of, 116,
    123
campus culture knowledge
    importance for, 118
campus life participation of, 116–17
campus security as team with, 113
CARE team management of, 119
centrality role of, 103
clearinghouse and doctor definition
    of, 118
close student connections and
    commitment of, 112
collaboration facilitation as, 105, 122
collaboration flexibility in, 106
collaboration suggestions for, 106
colleague differences relying on, 103
community development and,
    118–19
conduct concept in, 111
CSAO as pitfall guard for, 107
CSAO role alignment and
    differentiation in, 107, 123
deep knowledge base of, 108–9
direct report comment about, 107–8
diversity and inclusion praise for, 110
diversity and social justice and
    privilege knowledge importance
    for, 109–10, 122

fairness and consistency of, 115
flexibility limit of, 106–7
as generalist, 118
"hard job" colleague recognition of,
    121
individual and whole student
    advocacy of, 115, 123
individual student well-being
    concern of, 119
institutional context understanding
    of, 117
institutional knowledge base
    requirement of, 109, 123
institutional professionals and
    students responding to, 104
institutional value embodiment of,
    117
as institution citizen, 105–6
issues alternative approach
    exploration of, 106, 114
judgment ability of, 121
limited views on role of, 120
meaningful student relationships
    establishment of, 111
multipartiality leveraging of, 115
multiple perspectives advocating of,
    113
on personal qualities of, 121
problem-solving ability of, 121
relationship building as, 105, 117,
    122
resiliency of, 122, 123
response readability in, 105
role definition clarity in, 120, 123
as senior administration and staff
    members bridge, 107
shared problem-solving in, 106
staff morale maintaining of, 108
as staff support and advocate, 108
strong student relationships for,
    110
as student and administration bridge
    and balance, 113–14
student contact enjoyment of,
    122–23

Title IX compliance in, 67
Title IX intersection with, 65
University of Virginia sexual assault
complaint handling in, 66–67
student connections, 56, 73, 112, 128,
134, 169
The Student Personnel Point of View
(ACE), 149
students of concern teams, 62
suicide, 27, 51–52, 63–64, 81, 145

Talbot, Marion, 5–6
technology, 45, 91–92, 141–42, 145,
147
terminal degrees, 138
Diaz EdD decision in, 20
EdD as practice focused in, 20
field experience in, 19
Goldstein PhD decision in, 19–20
JD as, 20–21
legal and compliance issues impact
in, 21
PhD and EdD fields of study in, 19
PhD and EdD path differences in,
19
Rivera JD and master's pursuit in,
21–22
search firms regarding, 18–19
threat assessment teams, 62
Tinto, V., 71
Title IX, 1, 3, 4, 56, 66, 68–69
evolution of, 79–80
student conduct compliance and
intersection with, 65, 67
Twenty-Sixth Amendment, 148

United States (U.S.), 56, 58, 66–67
Department of Education's Office of
Civil Rights, 64
Department of Justice, 64
Supreme Court cases of, 57
University of California, Berkeley
as free speech hub, 56
Yiannopoulos's college tour and, 60

University of Colorado, Boulder
free speech and, 56
Yiannopoulos's college tour and, 61
University of Virginia, 66–67
University of Washington,
Yiannopoulos's college tour and,
60–61
U.S. *See* United States

Valverde, Leonard, 95
Varlotta, L., 37
VAWA. *See* Violence Against Women
Act
vicarious trauma phenomenon, 80, 81,
84
vice president of student affairs (VPSA),
127, 159–62, 164–65
Violence Against Women Act (VAWA),
68
"voice for students," 112–13, 128, 134
VPSA. *See* vice president of student
affairs

Western Michigan University, 64
White, Lori, 10
Wild, Rob, 84–85, 88, 90
Wolff, S. B., 48
Woodard, D., Jr., 34
Woods, E., 81–82
work-life integration (life skills
development), 15, 79
baby boomers work-style and, 85
boundary setting in, 97
burnout attrition study in, 82
burnout definition in, 81–82
communication technology burden
and benefit in, 89–90
community engagement and
university alignment for, 87–88
community engagement reflection
questions for, 88
compassion satisfaction in, 81
dean of students role evolving and,
79–80

Assessment and Accreditation Education books from Stylus Publishing

Leading Assessment for Student Success
Ten Tenets That Change Culture and Practice in Student Affairs
Edited by Rosie Phillips Bingham, Daniel Bureau, and Amber Garrison Duncan
Foreword by Marilee J. Bresciani Ludvik

A Leader's Guide to Competency-Based Education
From Inception to Implementation
Deborah J. Bushway, Laurie Dodge, and Charla S. Long
Foreword by Amy Laitinen

Enhancing Assessment in Higher Education
Putting Psychometrics to Work
Edited by Tammie Cumming and M. David Miller
Foreword by Michael J. Kolen

Coming to Terms With Student Outcomes Assessment
Faculty and Administrators' Journeys to Integrating Assessment in Their Work and Institutional Culture
Edited by Peggy L. Maki

Assessing for Learning
Edition 2
Building a Sustainable Commitment Across the Institution
Peggy L. Maki

Assessing and Improving Student Organizations
A Guide for Students
Brent D. Ruben and Tricia Nolfi

Gender and Higher Education books from Stylus Publishing

Answering the Call
African American Women in Higher Education Leadership
Beverly L. Bower and Mimi Wolverton

Women in Academic Leadership
Professional Strategies, Personal Choices
Edited by Diane R. Dean, Susan J. Bracken, and Jeanie K. Allen
Foreword by Claire Van Ummersen

Intersections of Identity and Sexual Violence on Campus
Centering Minoritized Students' Experiences
Edited by Jessica C. Harris and Chris Linder
Foreword by Wagatwe Wanjuki

Sisters of the Academy
Emergent Black Women Scholars in Higher Education
Edited by Reitumetse Mabokela and Anna L. Green

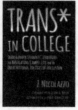

Trans* in College
Transgender Students' Strategies for Navigating Campus Life and the Institutional Politics of Inclusion
Z Nicolazzo
Foreword by Kristen A. Renn
Afterword by Stephen John Quaye

The Coach's Guide for Women Professors
Who Want a Successful Career and a Well-Balanced Life
Rena Seltzer
Foreword by Frances Rosenbluth

General Interest books from Stylus Publishing

Are You Smart Enough?
How Colleges' Obsession with Smartness Shortchanges Students
Alexander W. Astin

The New Science of Learning
How to Learn in Harmony With Your Brain
Terry Doyle and Todd D. Zakrajsek
Foreword by Kathleen F. Gabriel

Of Education, Fishbowls, and Rabbit Holes
Rethinking Teaching and Liberal Education for an Interconnected World
Jane Fried with Peter Troiano
Foreword by Dawn R. Person

Managing Your Professional Identity Online
A Guide for Faculty, Staff, and Administrators
Kathryn E. Linder
Foreword by Laura Pasquini

Teach Yourself How to Learn
Strategies You Can Use to Ace Any Course at Any Level
Saundra Yancy McGuire with Stephanie McGuire
Foreword by Mark McDaniel

Pitch Perfect
Communicating With Traditional and Social Media for Scholars, Researchers, and Academic Leaders
William Tyson
Foreword by Robert Zemsky

Graduate and Doctoral Education books from Stylus Publishing

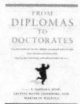

From Diplomas to Doctorates
The Success of Black Women in Higher Education and its Implications for Equal Educational Opportunities for All
Edited by V. Barbara Bush, Crystal Renee Chambers, and Mary Beth Walpole

The Latina/o Pathway to the Ph.D.
Abriendo Caminos
Edited by Jeanett Castellanos, Alberta M. Gloria, and Mark Kamimura
Foreword by Melba Vasquez and Hector Garza

On Becoming a Scholar
Socialization and Development in Doctoral Education
Jay Caulfield
Edited by Susan K. Gardner and Pilar Mendoza
Foreword by Ann E. Austin and Kevin Kruger

Developing Quality Dissertations in the Humanities
A Graduate Student's Guide to Achieving Excellence
Barbara E. Lovitts and Ellen L. Wert

Developing Quality Dissertations in the Sciences
A Graduate Student's Guide to Achieving Excellence
Barbara E. Lovitts and Ellen L. Wert

Developing Quality Dissertations in the Social Sciences
A Graduate Student's Guide to Achieving Excellence
Barbara E. Lovitts and Ellen L. Wert

The Department Chair as Transformative Diversity Leader Building
Inclusive Learning Environments in Higher Education
Edna Chun and Alvin Evans
Foreword by Walter H. Gmelch

Community Colleges as Incubators of Innovation
Unleashing Entrepreneurial Opportunities for Communities and Students Edited by Rebecca A. Corbin and Ron Thomas
Foreword by Andy Stoll, Afterword by J. Noah Brown

Contingent Academic Labor
Evaluating Conditions to Improve Student Outcomes
Daniel B. Davis
Foreword by Adrianna Kezar

Community College Leadership
A Multidimensional Model for Leading Change
Pamela L. Eddy
Foreword by George R. Boggs

College in the Crosshairs
An Administrative Perspective on Prevention of Gun Violence
Edited by Brandi Hephner LaBanc and Brian O. Hemphill
Foreword by Kevin Kruger and Cindi Love

Building the Field of Higher Education Engagement
Foundational Ideas and Future Directions
Edited by Lorilee R. Sandmann and Diann O. Jones

Online & Distance Learning books from Stylus Publishing

Discussion-Based Online Teaching To Enhance Student Learning
Second Edition
Theory, Practice and Assessment
Tisha Bender

Social Media for Active Learning
Engaging Students in Meaningful Networked Knowledge Activities
Vanessa Dennen

High-Impact Practices in Online Education
Research and Best Practices
Edited by Kathryn E. Linder and Chrysanthemum Mattison Hayes
Foreword by Kelvin Thompson

The Productive Online and Offline Professor
A Practical Guide
Bonni Stachowiak
Foreword by Robert Talbert

Jump-Start Your Online Classroom
Mastering Five Challenges in Five Days
David S. Stein and Constance E. Wanstreet

eService-Learning
Creating Experiential Learning and Civic Engagement Through Online and Hybrid Courses
Edited by Jean R. Strait and Katherine Nordyke
Foreword by Andrew Furco

Race & Diversity books from Stylus Publishing

Advancing Black Male Student Success From Preschool Through Ph.D.
Edited by Shaun R. Harper and J. Luke Wood

Everyday White People Confront Racial and Social Injustice
15 Stories
Edited by Eddie Moore, Jr., Marguerite W. Penick-Parks, and Ali Michael
Foreword by Paul C. Gorski

The Diversity Consultant Cookbook
Preparing for the Challenge
Written and Edited by Eddie Moore, Jr., Art Munin, and Marguerite W. Penick-Parks
Foreword by Jamie Washington, Afterword by Joey Iazzetto

Critical Race Spatial Analysis
Mapping to Understand and Address Educational Inequity
Edited by Deb Morrison, Subini Ancy Annamma, and Darrell D. Jackson

Closing the Opportunity Gap
Identity-Conscious Strategies for Retention and Student Success
Edited by Vijay Pendakur
Foreword by Shaun R. Harper

Bandwidth Recovery
Helping Students Reclaim Cognitive Resources Lost to Poverty, Racism, and Social Marginalization
Cia Verschelden
Foreword by Lynn Pasquerella

Student Affairs books from Stylus Publishing

Developing Effective Student Peer Mentoring Programs
A Practitioner's Guide to Program Design, Delivery, Evaluation, and Training
Peter J. Collier
Foreword by Nora Domínguez

The First Generation College Experience
Implications for Campus Practice, and Strategies for Improving Persistence and Success
Jeff Davis

Intersections of Identity and Sexual Violence on Campus
Centering Minoritized Students' Experiences
Edited by Jessica C. Harris and Chris Linder
Foreword by Wagatwe Wanjuki

A Guide to Becoming a Scholarly Practitioner in Student Affairs
Lisa J. Hatfield and Vicki L. Wise
Foreword by Kevin Kruger

Making Global Learning Universal
Promoting Inclusion and Success for All Students
Hilary Landorf, Stephanie Doscher, and Jaffus Hardrick
Foreword by Caryn McTighe Musil

Overcoming Educational Racism in the Community College
Creating Pathways to Success for Minority and Impoverished Student Populations
Edited by Angela Long
Foreword by Walter G. Bumphus

Student Affairs books from Stylus Publishing

Living-Learning Communities That Work
A Research-Based Model for Design, Delivery, and Assessment
Karen Kurotsuchi Inkelas, Jody E. Jessup-Anger, Mimi Benjamin, and Matthew R. Wawrzynski

Contested Issues in Troubled Times
Student Affairs Dialogues on Equity, Civility, and Safety
Edited by Peter M. Magolda, Marcia B. Baxter Magolda, and Rozana Carducci
Foreword by Lori Patton Davis

The Lives of Campus Custodians
Insights into Corporatization and Civic Disengagement in the Academy
Peter M. Magolda
Foreword by Jeffrey F. Milem

A Good Job
Campus Employment as a High-Impact Practice
George S. McClellan, Kristina L. Creager, and Marianna Savoca
Foreword by George D. Kuh

Debunking the Myth of Job Fit in Higher Education
Edited by Brian J. Reece, Vu T. Tran, Elliott N. DeVore, and Gabby Porcaro
Foreword by Stephen John Quaye

Closing the Opportunity Gap
Identity-Conscious Strategies for Retention and Student Success
Edited by Vijay Pendakur
Foreword by Shaun R. Harper

Study Abroad/International Education books from Stylus

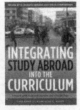

Integrating Study Abroad Into the Curriculum
Theory and Practice Across the Disciplines
Edited by Elizabeth Brewer and Kiran Cunningham
Foreword by Madeleine F. Greene

Integrating Worlds
How Off-Campus Study Can Transform Undergraduate Education
Scott D. Carpenter, Helena Kaufman, and Malene Torp
Foreword by Jane Edwards

Leading Internationalization
A Handbook for International Education Leaders
Edited by Darla K. Deardorff and Harvey Charles
Foreword by E. Gordon Gee
Afterword by Allen E. Goodman

Making Global Learning Universal
Promoting Inclusion and Success for All Students
Hillary Landorf, Stephanie Doscher, and Jaffus Hardrick
Foreword by Caryn McTighe Musil

Assessing Study Abroad
Theory, Tools, and Practice
Edited by Victor Savicki and Elizabeth Brewer
Foreword by Brian Whalen

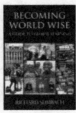

Becoming World Wise
A Guide to Global Learning
Richard Slimbach